How To Legally Obtain A Second Citizenship And Passport — And Why You Want To

Adam Starchild

Loompanics Unlimited
Port Townsend, Washington

Notice from the Author:

Seekers of a quick route to a second passport are often enticed by newspaper advertisements or directories purporting to list sources that sell instant citizenships. Unfortunately, in almost every case, there have been problems of legitimacy of the documents offered, and the firms eventually disappear. At the crude end of the business are firms that sell counterfeit documents, some of them very impressive indeed.

Next step up is the stolen document, and these schemes may last for some time, until the country concerned does an audit of its passport inventory and finds that either a consul or a passport office employee has been selling blanks. This has happened recently with both Ireland and the Dominican Republic.

At the most sophisticated end are the law firms who are bribing the local general in power to grant the citizenship. These documents may be valid somewhat longer, but there are still inherent problems — such as a new regime deciding that they were all illegally issued.

The simple truth — which many people don't want to believe — is that any advertised passport source that claims to offer instant citizenship without meeting the legal requirements of the country is not offering a genuine product. That's why you won't find a list of instant passport sources in this book, and the only addresses given are ones of unquestioned legitimacy that I won't be embarrassed to have readers ask me about some years in the future.

For a citizenship — and the implied second passport — to perform as you need it to, proper and genuine issue is essential. If you just want a phony document for your fugitive travels, there are cheaper and quicker ways to obtain one than to participate in a legitimate citizenship program.

Published by:
Loompanics Unlimited
PO Box 1197
Port Townsend, WA 98368
Loompanics Unlimited is a division of Loompanics Enterprises, Inc.

ISBN 1-55950-111-1
Library of Congress Card Catalog 94-73546

Contents

Introduction

Nationality law is one of the most confusing areas of international jurisprudence, primarily because law on nationality in different countries is extremely varied, based on individual histories, traditions, and legal concepts.

Anyone considering acquiring more than one nationality should proceed in full awareness of the risk of winding up with no nationality at all. You must proceed with care and, in all cases, seek well qualified legal advice. Obtaining accurate information can be difficult — different consulates of the same country often give different answers, which don't necessarily match the answers given by a citizenship lawyer within the country. Or there may be special clauses in the law with which the consulate is not familiar. Consulates deal with the everyday problems, such as children born in the territory served by the consulate of nationals of the home country, but that doesn't mean that they are familiar with every clause and loophole that may be in their citizenship law.

And many countries are reluctant to give general information for publication. They simply answer inquiries (if they answer at all) by saying that every case is different and the individuals concerned should visit the consulate and bring their documentation.

These difficulties are mentioned so that you will know to check and double check every possibility regarding your country of ancestry or that of your spouse. The first answer you get may not be the right one.

This book has been prepared primarily with U.S. citizens in mind. Many of our readers may be of other nationalities. They should be aware that international rules regarding dual citizenship vary from country to country. That means that if you are Dutch, for example, and interested in gaining a second passport, you must proceed in accordance with Dutch law. The consulate of your other nationality in the U.S. frequently can advise. Quite often consulates are better informed than lawyers in the home country on rules for current citizens, simply because they have to deal with these matters every day.

The main effect of the international legal confusion surrounding second passports and dual nationality is that some people have more than one nationality. And some people even have more passports than nationalities.

It is also possible to hold a country's passport without holding its nationality, as was the case for Costa Rica "pensionado" passport holders.

And many people in this world simply have no citizenship. Most are refugees, but a few are stateless for other reasons. These people may be able to obtain stateless persons' identity documents, but these usually require an advance visa for every country to be entered.

"What is a passport? Here is a reasonable definition. A passport, a printed permission signed by the secretary of state of the home department of a country, allows a subject of that country to leave and travel abroad. The system of passports has become much more rigid and vexatious during the last half-century. The only civilized countries in which passports are not required are the British Islands and the United States."

— Penny Cyclopedia, 1840

You can get a passport from any country whose nationality you hold, unless it is a country trying to keep its people from leaving (such as Vietnam). Of course, sometimes you can get other passports as well as those you are entitled to by nationality. Costa Rica was the best-known country to give what amounted to passports to people who were not its citizens (although in a strict legal sense it was a travel document and not a passport).

Chapter 1
A Brief History Of Passports And Nationality

T hough the passport is a very old idea, the U.S. passport is a very new one. The U.S. government wants people to think it is normal for a government to control the comings and goings of its citizenry. The fact of the matter is that passports were not required for travel abroad until quite recently.

Documents indicate that there was control of the frontiers of Egypt in the second millennium B.C., during the reign of Pharaoh Thutmos III. The United States was very late in *requiring* passports for entering and did not institute document control at its borders until 1921 (although passports were available prior to this).

In most of Western Europe, passports were instituted in the Napoleonic period. The Napoleonic Code reduced the right of nationality from what it had been in the heady days of the French Revolution.

Until 1906, it was perfectly legal to become a naturalized American without surrendering your previous passport. At the beginning of this century, naturalization usually signaled the end of travel for the foreign-born American; passports were unnecessary for the native-born citizen, who could re-enter the country simply by stating that he had been born in the U.S. After all, it was a land of immigrants, many of whom could not have provided documentation upon arrival in the United States.

The introduction of federal law in 1921 requiring passports was a by-product of concern about the loyalty of German-Americans during World War I. Many German-born immigrants settled in the U.S. and lived there for years without bothering to declare their nationality. (Those who did usually were religious dissenters.) Many kept their German nationality (as they were entitled to do if they were naturalized before 1906).

There also had been concern at one time about the loyalty of Irish-Americans (during the Mexican and Civil wars). At those times, however, the memory of the Alien and Sedition Acts, the fact that many people active in politics wanted to protect the foreign-born, and the country's economic needs were enough to prevent the enactment of any federal laws. The 1921 reforms were possible because they were associated with the simultaneous restriction on immigration.

Restrictions on naturalization and immigration often were justified in the McCarthy-McCarran years by claims that new Americans ("hyphenated Americans") were disloyal.

Likewise, in the 1950s, government attempts to tighten control on citizens were often justified by xenophobia and claims that the "Reds" were abusing their citizenship rights. In some cases, "communists" who had come to the United States as children were stripped of their U.S. naturalization and deported. Other native-born Americans were denied the right to travel by not being allowed passports. One of the most notable in this latter group was the actor/singer Paul Robeson.

Chapter 2
Acquisition Of Nationality

Y ou can obtain dual nationality in at least five ways: two forms of right of birth (both described below), and naturalization by residence, by merit, and by purchase. Under the laws of some countries, you can obtain their nationalities by marrying a citizen (often regardless of sex). You can get nationality by being the parent of a citizen in some countries (even by being the illegitimate parent of a citizen in some cases). And often you can gain entry or accelerated citizenship if you are a political or religious refugee or the offspring of refugees. These are the most realistic options, and the discussion will be limited to them.

For the record, however, you can obtain foreign nationality in other ways as well. You can obtain nationality by adoption, legitimation, or recognition of paternity, which is a special case. Under laws creating new countries, such as the incorporation of territory as the United States grew westward, the wholesale chopping up of the former Turkish and Austro-Hungarian empires after World War I, and the changes in the frontiers of Eastern Europe after World War II, collective and involuntary naturalization of the residents of these territories occurred. The same happened in the cases of Moslems in newly independent India and Israel in 1948. It also happened to Hindus in newly independent Pakistan. The world has had many problems as a result of these types of naturalization.

Nationality by Birth

As a result of being the home of immigrants, America is the biggest practitioner of the principle in nationality law that lawyers call *jus soli,* the right to nationality by virtue of place of birth, which is still the dominant factor in U.S. nationality law. The opposing principle, *jus sanguinis,* is the right to nationality by virtue of "blood," i.e., ancestry. Nationality law in most countries is a mixture of these two notions.

Most of Europe currently operates under *jus sanguinis,* but with exceptions. The most important of these involve people who otherwise would be born without a country, i.e.: apatrides. This provides opportunities.

Many countries which want to foster immigration or which used to want to foster immigration are in the *jus soli* group. Among these are Canada, Australia, and many Latin American countries. In Europe, under the pressure of immigration, even countries which used to allow some elements of *jus soli*, such as France and Britain, have now reduced them.

Some countries still provide citizenship to virtually anyone born in their territories: the United States, Canada, Ireland, Israel, Jamaica, Bolivia, Mexico, and Brazil. Other countries have residence requirements which are enforced with varying severity, either on the parents if they are not nationals (Italy requires that the parents have lived in Italy 10 years before the child was born unless one of the parents or grandparents is or was Italian), or on the child born to parents who are not nationals prior to his or her being given the country's nationality (Denmark, France, and Belgium, theoretically for periods from 16 to 18 years). Residence requirements on newborn babies or their parents may apply.

Still other countries *only* grant nationality to children born in their territories who otherwise would be stateless, precisely to avoid dual nationality. (Finland is an example.) Some countries concerned with racial purity, notably Japan, have carefully worded laws which deny nationality to those who just happen to be born there — generation after generation. Thus third-generation Japanese-born Koreans are still not Japanese citizens.

Naturalization by Residence

In the American colonies, naturalization was left to the individual colonies and often involved religious and financial tests. Under the first article of the U.S. Constitution, Congress was given the power to "establish a uniform rule of naturalization." The statute of 1790 provided that those of foreign birth could become American. It was based on the individual's right to expatriate himself from the nationality he had been born with — a concept which was unfortunately not recognized by Anglo-Saxon Common Law.

Congress also declared to be citizens those born outside the United States to citizen fathers who themselves had lived in the U.S. *(jus sanguinis).*

These notions were tinkered with in the 19th century, but not substantially changed. And they were administered by the separate states.

With the 14th Amendment in 1868, the United States adopted the notion of *jus soli*. Even if your parents were not citizens (usually because they were slaves), you were a citizen by right of having been born on American soil and having been emancipated. The text reads "all persons born or naturalized in the United States, and subject to the jurisdiction thereof, are citizens of the United States and the state wherein they reside." (The Indians were a special case.)

As the United States gained territory from foreign countries, citizenship was conferred on the people who came with it: Michigan (1794, formerly British); the Louisiana Purchase (1803); and Florida (1819); former Mexican territories (1848-1853); the U.S. Virgin Islands (1916, formerly Danish), and Puerto Rico (1917 for citizenship, although Puerto Rico was acquired from Spain in 1898). From 1918 to 1920, Filipinos were made U.S. citizens under the treaty with Spain — automatically and without giving the individual Filipino any say in the matter. People in territories that had belonged to no foreign state were also automatically naturalized, as were people in Alaska and Hawaii who had been Russian or Hawaiian citizens before U.S. annexation.

Aliens of European background were naturalized from 1790 by the separate states. The procedure involved applying as an immigrant upon arrival in the U.S. After five years of uninterrupted residency, the immigrants went before a judge with two American witnesses to swear an oath of loyalty. And they were given a Naturalization Certificate (after paying a fee). The procedure remains similar today.

Naturalization was extended to blacks in 1868, although in the Deep South, only after 1960 were many blacks treated as citizens (and permitted to vote and serve on juries, for example). Naturalization was extended to other races only in 1940. People of Chinese, Japanese, or Indian subcontinent backgrounds were barred from citizenship until then.

Naturalization by Merit

In 1793, as an expression of revolutionary enthusiasm, the French National Assembly virtually invited any foreigner who wanted to, to become French. "Any foreigner aged over 21, who has been domiciled in France for more than a year, or who lives here by his or her work, or who has acquired a property, or who has married a Frenchman or Frenchwoman, or who has adopted a child, or who supports an aged person, or who is deemed by the legislative body to be worthy of humane treatment *(d'avoir bien merite de humanite)* is admitted to the exercise of the rights of citizenship."

The tradition was thereby established of granting citizenship to those of merit or those who made an economic contribution to the country. This notion goes beyond either of the recognized principles of nationality law, and it is not studied by jurists.

Early beneficiaries included Thomas Paine, the British-born American revolutionary, who actually became such a good Frenchman in French eyes that he served as a member of the National Assembly for Calais. Along with other non-French deputies, he was imprisoned by the Jacobins, but managed to avoid the guillotine. A Dutchman, Anarcharsis Clootz, was also a National Assemblyman. But he was less lucky than Paine — he was guillotined for opposing Robespierre.

The United States does not grant citizenship to people because of merit (except by special Act of Congress), but it does give them priority in getting a visa. The visa category H1 covers workers of "distinguished merit or ability;" the category H2 covers workers performing services unavailable in the U.S.; the category H4 covers the spouses and children of these people. Furthermore, the visa category L1 covers inter-company transferees in executive, managerial, or specialized fields, and L2 covers their spouses and minor children.

Sometimes nationality by merit can just be a matter of being lucky enough to be in the right place at the right time. About 30 visiting French writers, politicians, journalists and entertainers were granted Lebanese citizenship in 1989 for expressing sympathy with the country's plight. Christian army commander Major-General Michael Aoun presented passports to the delegation.

Nationality by Checkbook

The idea of giving nationality by merit lives on, but it has been debased from its revolutionary beginnings. In many countries south of the border, you can in effect buy nationality through programs that are designed to attract investors to the country.

Under the 1945 Constitution, the law in Bolivia says that you can become Bolivian after two years' residence. This is "reduced to one year if your spouse is Bolivian, or your child is, or if you own real estate in the country, or if you have introduced an industry or invention of value to the community, or if you teach school, or operate a railroad." You automatically become Bolivian if you perform military service.

This is an extreme example of nationality by merit or service to the country, but many other countries operate under similar principles that have been turned into a simple matter of parting with cash. This is usually done through "making an investment" in an approved program, or buying an approved farm, but you don't really expect your "investment" to be recoverable. The Bolivian one costs about $20,000.

U.S. nationality can never be bought. The closest the U.S. comes to such programs is a special millionaires' residence visa for those investing $1 million or more (and creating a minimum number of jobs) in the U.S. U.S. immigration law provides for two categories of persons who have priority in obtaining visas for themselves, their spouses, and their children: E1 for "treaty traders" and E2 for "treaty investors." But these are non-resident visas, meaning that the time in the U.S. on the visa does not count toward the required residency for obtaining citizenship. They are intended for long term, but still temporary, business stays, even though they can generally be renewed indefinitely.

This type of business visa, or some close equivalent, is available in most countries. This book is concerned with obtaining a second citizenship, not residence.

Naturalization by Marriage

The 19th century adopted the notion, invented by the Napoleonic Code as far as the law books are concerned, of "the unity of the family." What this meant was that in some cases a woman had to give up her own nationality when she married a foreigner.

The United States, a land of immigrants, did not apply this notion during the 19th century. The 1855 U.S. Nationality Act specifically allowed alien women to become American upon marriage to a citizen — but nothing was said about the reverse.

However, as American nativism and xenophobia increased, the law was changed. In 1907, the U.S. Nationality Act read that "any American woman who marries a foreigner shall take the nationality of her husband." The result was heartbreak, injustice, and outrage.

A mere 15 years later, the so-called Cable Act of 1922 introduced the principle that "marriage has no effect on citizenship" for Americans. But in fact, the new law required that any American woman marrying an alien had to reapply for citizenship and wait a year; women who married the wrong sort of aliens lost their citizenship forever. Marriage to a man ineligible for citizenship on grounds of race was expatriating for U.S. women.

In 1934, the United States revised the Nationality Act to "lift requirements for spouses of Americans otherwise qualified" for citizenship. Once again, you got to become a citizen — at once — by marrying an American. On condition you were white or black. The race tests were removed in 1940.

But in 1940, with war on the horizon, American politicians began to worry that they had made things too easy for potential foreign spies. So a residency requirement was reintroduced. If a foreigner spent one year living in the United States with his or her American spouse, he or she could become a citizen. During the McCarthy years, a new wave of nativism overtook this law, and the residency requirement was raised to three years (either before or after the marriage).

Under current American law, spouses do not transmit citizenship, although marriage does make it easier for spouses of Americans to obtain both U.S. visas and U.S. citizenship — you get the visa (theoretically) automatically and citizenship in three years of residence rather than the regular five years. This is why the government snoops so hard to determine if these "mixed marriages" are real. The "automatic" visa can actually be very hard to obtain, and immigration officers will tend to ask all sorts of trick questions of the spouses separately to see if it is a marriage of convenience.

Marriage gives you French nationality after one year of marriage, whether in or out of France, but a French language test is also required. Marriage accelerates the naturalization process in countries from Brazil to Britain, from Bolivia to New Zealand.

In France, and some other European countries as well, traces of the revolutionary system remained in the 19th century; one could still become French by marrying a Frenchman. (Napoleon removed the idea that you could also become French by marrying a Frenchwoman.) In the 19th century, as a more patriarchal approach to marriage took hold, this rule was generalized, so that wives were expected to take their husbands' nationality.

Nowadays, thanks to a more egalitarian view of marriage and a United Nations convention that prohibits asymmetry in the assignment of nationality between spouses (to which the United States and most Western countries adhere), many marriages between people with different nationalities result in dual nationality for the children of such unions. (This is explained in further detail below.)

In many cases, mixed marriages also give both spouses the nationality of the other quite painlessly (or at least more rapidly).

In Ireland the non-Irish spouse can become a citizen after three years of marriage even though never having resided in Ireland. All that is necessary is to present the passports of both spouses and an affidavit by the Irish spouse that the marriage is still in effect, and the citizenship is granted automatically by registration. This can even be done at the nearest Irish consulate or embassy — it is not necessary to go to Ireland. Note that this is citizenship by registration, not naturalization. It therefore is not addressed by the U.S. laws on acquiring a second nationality by naturalization. It is also not a discretionary process in Irish law but a matter of right. This latter point is important. Many countries reduce or waive the residence requirement for naturalization of a spouse, but the other legal requirements still have to be met, such as speaking the language, being of good moral character, not having a criminal record, etc. But in the case of citizenship by registration, there is no bureaucratic discretion to refuse the citizenship.

Some countries only allow those who acquired their nationality by birth to pass it on to their spouses.

The Citizenship of Married Women

The rules concerning spouses acquiring nationality generally are or were sexually asymmetrical.

The constant tinkering with U.S. rules of citizenship and marriage between 1922 and 1940 was characteristic of the period, and there were virtually as many changes in the law in other Western countries. Tracing French law regarding transmission of citizenship to spouses is equally confusing, and the twists and turns of British law also have been summarized. All this tinkering was going on precisely at the time that the international lawyers were trying to standardize rules. But the tenor of legal changes was that women were increasingly being given the right to maintain their nationalities even if they married foreigners. In short, many countries were beginning to break with the Napoleonic idea of family unity. And of course, many children with dual nationalities were being born to these mixed marriages.

It was during this period of rapidly changing nationality law that the first conference on trying to resolve the matter of dual nationality took place, in 1930, in The Hague. International lawyers were as confused as the lawmakers in the United States during this period. On the one hand, they talked about family unity (and in effect tried to weed out dual nationality before the little children who might have it were even conceived); on the other hand, there were countries that were becoming convinced that women might be citizens, too. Thanks to the problem of how to determine the nationality of women married to foreigners, the League of Nations system was unable to come to a conclusion about eliminating dual nationality.

It was only one year after the 1930 Hague Convention failed utterly to address the question, as jurists pontificated about Freedom of the Wife versus Unity of the Family, that the women's movement took up the question. In 1931, the International Women's Movement adopted a resolution that "there shall be no distinction based on sex in law relating to nationality" and "marriage shall not affect the nationality of husband, wife, or child."

The first success of this program came in 1935, when the Convention of Montevideo (which grouped the American states) virtually adopted the language of the Women's Movement. The Conference Article 7 read, "Neither matrimony nor its dissolution affects the nationality of the husband, or wife, or their children."

This was highly theoretical, because the United States and other countries did not change their laws. In 1948, the Universal Declaration of Human Rights of the United Nations got into the question, although the declaration was not legally binding on U.N. member countries either. Article 15 said, "No one shall be arbitrarily deprived of his nationality nor denied the right to change his nationality." ("His" under international law includes "her.") "Arbitrarily" was defined so as to include the meaning "as a result of marriage."

Many countries refuse to adopt symmetry in nationality law between the sexes, despite signing the U.N. declaration. The Egyptian delegate, pressed by the then-president of the General Assembly, Mme. Pandit, argued that "it is customary for a woman to agree, upon marrying an alien, that her children shall be of the father's nationality." It is reported that she glared at him. The Inter-American Court of Justice (which judges the Montevideo Convention) backed asymmetry as recently as 1984 (Judgments and Opinions 84, Number 4, Paragraph 44): "the provision which favors only one of the spouses does not constitute discrimination," ruled the judges.

The non-binding declaration became binding in 1953 on countries that chose to make it so. Unlike its generally rotten record for ratifying international human rights rules, the United States accepts that passport rights relating to marriage are sexually neutral. The language of the 1931 Women's Movement text became a U.N. Resolution from the U.N. Commission on the Status of Women, "There shall be no distinction based on sex in law relating to nationality."

The United Nations loves to pass more resolutions than are needed to prove its virtue. So, in 1979, it produced The Convention on the Elimination of All Forms of Discrimination Against Women, which went into effect in 1981. (The United States signed in 1980.) Article 9 "provides for equal rights for women regarding the status of their nationality and ...the nationality of their children." However, not all member countries of the international organization have decided to ratify that resolution or revise their domestic laws to fit it. And most legal systems have not redefined nationality retroactively. So if your grandmother was expatriated for marrying the wrong fellow, you cannot claim that it was a sexist decision three generations later and try to reclaim your citizenship from the government in question.

Under national and international law, a series of rules have won wide acceptance (although they are not formalized by treaty). One is that people may not be deprived of nationality by governments against their will. The language is incorporated in Article 15 of the U.N. Declaration on Human Rights. It has strongly influenced U.S. case law since then.

Great Britain is a signatory. But it has not adopted any special measures for the Hong Kong-Chinese, who most assuredly do not want to cease being British against their will. (The British argue that they are colonial subjects, not citizens. The United States used a similar argument regarding Puerto Ricans until 1917, when it suddenly made them citizens; cynical Puerto Ricans say it was so they could be drafted in World War I.)

Diplomats' Children Under jus soli

By law, the United States does not grant citizenship to the children of diplomats or U.N. officials who happen to be born in the U.S. However, in practice, many such children do get U.S. nationality, because their mothers as opposed to their fathers do not make a point of declaring their diplomatic status. Unless the mother makes a big thing of her status, the child born in the United States is presumed to be a citizen, and gets a birth certificate that allows him or her to be issued a passport.

The treatment of diplomatic offspring goes back to the French Revolution. Even when the United States and Britain practiced *jus soli*, diplomatic offspring and those of a foreign occupying power were excluded by law. Now international law reinforces this tradition. By practice, as in the United States, the presumption of nationality by birth still overrides a specific exclusion for diplomats, simply because the birth certificate is not marked in any special way to indicate that the child was not a citizen — even if the registrar of births was aware of the situation.

The children of diplomats and international civil servants born in France were at one time granted the right to French nationality under certain conditions. This idea, which dates back to the French Revolution, managed to survive Napoleon's switch to the *jus sanguinis* camp. However, France abolished this tradition by becoming a signatory to the 1930 Hague Convention, which excludes diplomats from *jus soli*. But in practice, as in the U.S., it is difficult for those registering births to keep an eye out for diplomatic offspring.

Some countries are not signatories to the 1930 Hague Convention, or refuse to conform to its rules. In Bolivia today, under the 1945 Constitution, which post-dates the Hague Convention, children born to diplomats stationed there are automatically given Bolivian citizenship.

In contrast to American law, many countries practicing *jus sanguinis* grant their nationalities and passports to the offspring of their citizens, wherever they may be born. So it is possible to be a citizen of many countries without ever having set foot in any of them.

Residence Requirements

In 1809, the Napoleonic Code got rid of the rampant distribution of citizenship by merit. Yet even the restrictive new French system did not require that French nationals live in France. Logically, being French was inherited, so it did not matter if you actually lived there. France only instituted a residence requirement for citizenship in 1921, and it merely applied to naturalized Frenchmen, not to those who became French at birth. France was even slower than the United States in requiring passports from its own citizens; France required that Frenchmen returning to the country show passports only after 1928.

In contrast, countries receiving immigrants have always imposed a residence requirement before naturalization — and sometimes even after naturalization. It normally takes five years of U.S. residence under a legal alien registration card to become a citizen. There also may be a quiz on government and civic structure, and a requirement that the potential citizen be able to read and write English.

Only in recent years has the United States removed rules (dating from 1921 and repeated in laws in the following decade) whereby naturalized Americans who returned to their countries of origin lost their U.S. nationality. If you were a naturalized U.S. citizen, it used to be that you could not spend more than a few weeks in your country of origin without putting your U.S. citizenship at risk. In 1952, the Supreme Court *(Rosenberg v. Fleutl)* ruled against the residence test on naturalized Americans, but it took a while before the law was changed. And the new law was not retroactive. People who had lost their citizenship under the old law did not get it back unless they sued.

Similarly, only lately has the United States gotten rid of the residence requirement on children born to one American and one foreign parent outside the United States. These offspring used to have to meet quite stringent rules on residence before they turned 23 years old (18, initially) so as not to lose their U.S. citizenship. This reform did not apply to those who had lost their citizenship under the old law.

Residence before naturalization was required by the United States from 1790. It also was required *after* naturalization if the U.S. citizen wished to transmit his nationality to his children.

The reason for residence restrictions applying to new citizens in the United States was a fear that generations of pseudo-Americans might be bred in non-English-speaking countries. All it would take was one fellow who had spent five years in the United States, and then returned to his homeland and had a bunch of children (American citizens because of papa), who then in turn would marry and have children, etc., creating whole mobs of American citizens with scant ties to the U.S. (Only papa is mentioned as an example because, during the inter-War period, paternal but not maternal assignment of citizenship was common.)

Foreign countries also impose residence requirements on applicants for naturalization. The shortest residence requirement is zero, which is the case for Jews immigrating to Israel. (Note that Israel has very steep taxes and a draft applying to both men and women. As a result, even those who are stateless, such as the Soviet Jews, often scheme to get any nationality other than Israeli.)

Countries where citizenship can be bought tend to waive residence requirements. However, the danger is that these citizenships may be lost in the event of a political changeover, or just that the appropriate general doesn't stay bribed. For that reason this book stresses citizenships that are available through other methods such as inheritance and marriage, or well established and approved investor-immigrant programs.

Relatively short residence requirements are used by many countries that want to encourage immigration. Many countries reduce the requirement in the case of anyone who makes an economic contribution to the country by investment or who marries a citizen. Even countries that do not welcome new immigrants frequently cut residence requirements for those who marry their nationals, to promote family unity.

Canada has a three-year residence requirement, which is strictly enforced.

Five years to seven years is the norm for most countries. Some countries that want to discourage immigration use a longer period. Switzerland uses twelve years; Germany uses 10 years.

Commonwealth Residence Credits

Many Commonwealth countries allow a reduced period of residence by granting credit for residence in other Commonwealth countries. Thus a citizen of an African Commonwealth country may have a fairly easy time obtaining citizenship in a West Indies Commonwealth country. This rule applies to anyone, not just a citizen of a Commonwealth country. For example, an American who has lived in Canada for a few years may be able to credit those years towards part of the residence requirement for a Jamaican passport (although the last couple of years nearly always have to be actual residence in the country that is going to grant the citizenship). But should you be considering citizenship in a Commonwealth country, be sure to obtain a copy of the citizenship law and read it carefully with a view to these possible loopholes — it is impossible to cover all of them in this book. Before spending money on a lawyer, write to the country concerned and purchase a copy of the law from their government printing office. Since these are Commonwealth countries the laws are all printed in English.

Residence Requirements for U.S. Citizens

The United States does not like its citizens to live abroad. In 1790, the law allowed only one generation of children born to American fathers abroad (regardless of the nationality of the mothers — this was the 18th century, after all) to retain citizenship. Where grandfathers were Americans, fathers were American. But if the fathers never resided in the United States, *their* children were not American.

This curious residence requirement on citizens by birth lasted and lasted and lasted. It still does. It shows the distrust of American legislators for *jus sanguinis,* and the fear that without contact with the American earth and air and population, people will somehow lose their American essence.

In 1934, to show a new sexual equality, American mothers could transmit nationality even if residing abroad and married to foreigners. But the residence requirement was retained. Unless one of the parents of the foreign-born half-American child had resided in the United States for at least five years immediately before the parent was 18, that parent could not transmit nationality to the little one. Instead of only American grandfathers winding up with little foreign grandchildren against their will, American grandmothers could as well (via either their sons or their daughters).

In 1940 the residence requirement was doubled; a parent had to reside in the United States for at least 10 rather than five years to transmit nationality to a child born abroad whose other parent was a foreigner. (However, under the new law, the child himself had an easier time becoming American if he chose to live in the United States.)

Residence Requirements for Native-born Americans

As already discussed, earlier legislation had already introduced the idea of a residence requirement applying to native-born Americans (that is to say those born in the United States) in the matter of transmission of nationality. But in 1940, the government decided to impose a residency requirement on its native-born citizens in the matter of their own nationality. The 1940 law read, "if a child born in the United States enters the foreign state where he or either of his parents were a national and if he remains there more than six months" he is considered to have expatriated himself.

The law was intended to crack down on dual nationals born in the United States to foreign mothers who made the ocean crossing from troubled Europe to have U.S. citizen babies. But it had the effect in six months of ending the U.S. citizenship of children born in the U.S. to naturalized American mothers or fathers who happened subsequently to live in the country where the non-American parent had been born. Furthermore, if a naturalized American lived in the country where he or one of his parents was born, he also lost his citizenship in six months. The predictable outcome was that protesting Americans besieged their consulates in foreign lands.

A procedure was developed whereby if the American parent or the American child could prove that he had not entered a foreign army or accepted employment in the government service of a foreign state (specific expatriating acts), his citizenship was returned. The burden of proof, of course, was on the person claiming citizenship.

In 1952, despite the rise of xenophobia in the United States, the rule was eliminated by a new law. A presumed dual national, born to one American parent overseas, was allowed to live up to three years in a foreign country without losing his nationality. On the first day of year three he was required to visit a U.S. embassy and swear under oath that he wanted to retain his American citizenship. If the idea of swearing in a bunch of three-year-olds sounds ridiculous, recall that parents naturalizing children with themselves also swear an oath on the children's behalf.

The U.S. Oath of Citizenship

The United States requires that new citizens by naturalization swear an oath that requires that they give up any prior citizenship. If they swear falsely they lose their U.S. citizenship. The effect is to eliminate dual nationality. The oath reads as follows:

"I hereby declare, on oath, that I absolutely and entirely renounce and abjure all allegiance and fidelity to any foreign prince, potentate, state, or sovereignty, of whom or which I have heretofore been a subject or citizen; that I will support and defend the Constitution and laws of the United States of America against all enemies, foreign and domestic; that I will bear true faith and allegiance to the same; (that I will bear arms on behalf of the United States of America when required by law; that I will perform noncombatant service in the armed forces of the United States of America when required by law; that I will perform work of national importance under civilian direction when required by law;) and that I take this obligation freely without any mental reservation or purpose of evasion: so help me God." (The clauses in parentheses are now optional.)

Some other countries require similar oaths of naturalized citizens. However, despite such an oath renouncing former citizenships, the actual loss of citizenship is determined by the country of the original citizenship. Many cases of dual nationality result simply because the first country does not recognize anything other than an oath taken before one of its consular officers, or perhaps does not permit renunciation of citizenship at all.

Western Hemisphere Preference

Some groups of countries (the EU, the Benelux countries, and the Nordic group, for example) try to make it easier for folks living nearby to travel and work there. The countries of the Americas have attempted to create a system of preferences for immigrant visas. But hard economic facts have got in the way of ideals in this area.

Following are examples of inter-American preference: Bolivia admits Argentines with identification and without passports; Brazil exempts Argentines, Paraguayans, and Uruguayans from passport requirements; Chile admits U.S. citizens without passports; Costa Rica admits any holder of a tourist card; the Dominican Republic exempts U.S. and Canadian nationals with proof of identity from passport requirements; Ecuador exempts holders of tourist cards from passport requirements; El Salvador exempts U.S. citizens and Canadians with round-trip airline tickets from passport requirements; Guatemala exempts U.S. citizens and Canadians with tourist cards from passport requirements; Haiti does not require U.S. nationals or Canadians with birth certificates to have passports; Paraguay exempts citizens of Argentina, Brazil, Uruguay, and Chile who possess identification papers from showing passports; the United States exempts citizens of Mexico who enter from Mexico or Canada and hold a valid border-crossing card from passport requirements. Canadians who reside in Bermuda or Canada and who arrive in the United States after a visit anywhere in the Western Hemisphere or directly from Canada are exempt from passport requirements; and Venezuela exempts U.S. citizens with tourist cards from passport requirements. Tourist or transit cards are issued by airlines or the consul and normally do not require photographs. They are valid for 30 days to six months (depending on the country), are renewable, and normally are issued at little or no cost.

Chapter 3
The Advantages Of Multiple Nationality

W hy would anyone be interested in obtaining dual nationality?

If you cannot get a U.S. passport for some reason, having the right to another can be very useful. People in the United States can be denied passports to leave the country for the following reasons: being under a court order of parole or probation; being the subject of a federal warrant for arrest; being under subpoena by a federal grand jury; being in debt to the Internal Revenue Service (IRS) or another body of the federal government; and being declared mentally incompetent.

The U.S. practice on loss of nationality has changed a number of times since World War II, even though the statute has not. After decades of revoking the citizenship of persons who had been naturalized in a foreign country (as the statute requires), the State Department now ignores foreign naturalization unless there is additional evidence of an *intent* to lose U.S. citizenship. This could actually be a very delicate problem for a person who was naturalized abroad during the time of the earlier policy and believed that they were no longer a citizen, only to suddenly find that they are a citizen and owe U.S. taxes for the entire period. (There has not been such a case, but it is theoretically possible because of this change.)

The ONLY definitive ruling on loss of U.S. citizenship is made by the State Department issuing a certificate of loss of U.S. nationality. This is automatic in the case of a formal renunciation of citizenship, but it can also follow such acts as participating voluntarily in a foreign military service or being naturalized abroad with the intent to lose U.S. citizenship. While your U.S. citizenship may be open to challenge because of one of these acts, unless such a certificate has been issued, you may still be a U.S. citizen.

Norman Dacey, the famed author of *How To Avoid Probate*, held Irish nationality because of ancestry. He moved to Ireland some years ago and said that he was no longer a U.S. citizen. However, he never followed the required procedure of a formal renunciation of citizenship, and the Internal Revenue Service seized his U.S. book royalties on the grounds that he owed taxes and penalties for the years he had been living in Ireland without filing U.S. tax returns. He has since formally renounced U.S. citizenship.

Nothing you do in the United States can cause a loss of citizenship, so if you are naturalized by a foreign country through a mail-order citizenship, you do not lose U.S. citizenship by that act — BUT if you then reside abroad, that could create the required intent to lose citizenship under the statute.

You are now required to give your social security number to obtain a U.S. passport. This is an effort to increase enforcement of the law requiring tax returns and payments from all U.S. citizens. Congress was convinced — whether or not accurately

— that there were a couple of million Americans abroad who were not filing and paying U.S. taxes.

A second passport can save your life if you are unfortunate enough to be on an airplane that is hijacked by terrorists with a grievance against Uncle Sam — and most terrorists have a grievance against Uncle Sam.

There are other advantages as well. In many countries it is difficult for foreigners to obtain a work permit. It is often even more difficult for Americans to do so because of reciprocity rules in many countries. The U.S. is one of the most difficult places in the world to obtain a work permit, so foreign countries retaliate against American executives. Many American-based multinational corporations now make a point of hiring (or combing their existing staffs for) executives who have dual nationality so that they have the right to work in some other country as a citizen.

In the European Union (EU), citizens of any one of the member countries (Belgium, Denmark, France, Germany, Greece, Ireland, Italy, Luxembourg, Netherlands, Portugal, Spain, and the United Kingdom) have the right to live and work in any other member country without permits. Large American corporations are very interested in anyone who may be a citizen of one of these countries for these prized assignments. Many times the corporations urge executives to check on whether they might be a dual national without being aware of it, as is the case with many who had a father born in one of those countries (or in the case of Ireland, any one of the four grandparents).

In a great many countries, including Greece, Mexico, and Switzerland, foreigners are not allowed to buy real estate in certain restricted areas. Having local nationality is an advantage. And finding a loan to finance a real estate purchase in any country is always easier for a national, because most banks distrust foreigners.

In the United States foreigners are forbidden to control companies in sensitive industries. (For instance, foreign ownership of broadcasting companies, military suppliers, utilities, and railroads is prohibited in the U.S.) Similar rules apply in many other countries, and the prohibited list of industries may be much broader.

It is often difficult to purchase foreign securities — Eurobonds, offshore mutual funds, unit trusts, investment funds, SICAVs, or South African gold stocks — if all you have is U.S. citizenship. Only a very few large foreign companies have registered to sell their securities in the United States. Foreign brokers will not sell you unregistered securities, for fear of the Securities and Exchange Commission (SEC). If you want to own these securities, it helps to have a foreign identity and a foreign mailing address.

In addition, some foreign countries limit the right of foreigners to buy securities or certain classes of securities in their markets. Unless you have the right nationality, you may not be able to benefit from the best deals. Among the countries that limit foreigners' rights to purchase securities are Switzerland, Italy, Brazil, Taiwan, and South Korea. And in Switzerland, any non-Swiss opening a normal bank account is subject to a 35% withholding tax.

By purchasing and selling U.S. stocks and bonds with a foreign passport, it is possible to evade U.S. capital gains tax entirely (but be warned, this is illegal if you have retained U.S. nationality). On the other hand, you will be subject to a withholding tax on interest and dividends, usually 30% (but sometimes 0% or 15% if the country of your new nationality has a tax treaty with the U.S.). That withholding tax does not apply to U.S. bank account interest.

In some countries, such as Great Britain, college tuition is lower for those with that nationality. And some countries, including the United States, allow only their citizens to qualify for free education at military academies or other schools.

Having a second passport sometimes can help you acquire a more desirable third passport. An example is using an Israeli passport to get a German or a Spanish passport. Both countries make special arrangements for descendants of Jews who were driven from their countries (by the Nazis for Germany or by the Inquisition in 1492 for Spain).

A purchased Latin American nationality can ease acquisition of Spanish nationality. Similarly, a Brazilian passport can ease your way to Portuguese nationality, as of 1995. This may not continue for long, as both Spain and Portugal are under European Union (EU) pressure to drop the preference they give their former colonies in Latin America. Because Spain, Portugal, and Germany are in the European Union (formerly the European Community), having any one of these nationalities gives you the right to work and live without permits in any one of the EU countries.

Having a foreign nationality in addition to U.S. nationality does not allow you to avoid any of the U.S. taxes you otherwise would have to pay; nor does it allow you to get around or to evade the U.S. laws requiring reporting of large transfers of cash and securities overseas. Nor does foreign nationality in conjunction with U.S. citizenship allow you to avoid the law requiring that you report overseas securities or bank accounts in which $10,000 or more is held at any time. As long as you retain your U.S. citizenship, you must observe U.S. tax and reporting laws.

Chapter 4
The Disadvantages
Of Dual Nationality

There are disadvantages to having more than one nationality. The main problem is that many countries still have a draft, and young men may be called up by their foreign countries of nationality. Among the countries with a draft are France, Switzerland, and Israel. And international courts tend to uphold the rights of either nationality to impose military service on citizens of dual nationality. This is a serious enough problem that the U.S. military forces have policies prohibiting stationing a serviceman in a country where he might be considered a dual national (for example because he had a parent born in France).

In the event of a divorce, small children who have dual nationality by right of their parents' mixed marriage can easily be abducted by one parent, thereby denying the other custody or visitation rights. There are tens of thousands of cases every year of children who are abducted from their U.S. parents, particularly from U.S. mothers married to Moslem fathers from North Africa or the Middle East. Another country often involved in custody fights is Israel (whose very easy issuance of passports to Jews has been abused by escaping spouses of both sexes).

Another disadvantage results from the inheritance and estate tax laws of multiple jurisdictions. It is often difficult to avoid having more than one country tax the estate of a dual national.

For international lawyers, on the other hand, the disadvantages result from laws on trading with the enemy in time of war and the right of redress in international court. International and U.S. courts generally treat the holder of both an enemy and a third-country passport as if he were from the enemy country only. Also, multiple passport holders generally are not allowed to use the second nationality to sue the first country under international law.

Who Decides Whether You Can Be Drafted?

Under international law, the country where a dual national is living has the right to assert its claim to him without any interference from the other. In other words, you cannot use one of your nationalities to protect yourself from demands placed on you by your other nationality. The United States protested without any effect against the Swiss habit of granting Swiss nationality to those who were born to persons of Swiss origin generations before, and then drafting them. The Department of State in 1897 wrote to protest:

"There seems to be no end to the chain of inherited subjection ...if the Swiss premise is admitted, for if a native born son of a citizen of the United States can be claimed by Switzerland as a citizen because his father was formerly a

Switzer, the grandson and the descendants of the remotest generations may ...be claimed as Swiss citizens."

During World War I, the United States was unable to prevent Italy and Switzerland from drafting persons who had acquired U.S. nationality by naturalization and had returned to their original country.

While the Swiss finally backed off (in the 1950s!), later U.S. court rulings allowed Americans to be drafted and not lose American citizenship.

This may not be very good news for the person thereby deemed a dual national, however. Many would prefer not to serve in the army of any nation. And almost everyone would prefer not to be hanged. Following World War II, a Mr. Kawakita became vulnerable for a charge of treason for actions he took while wearing the Japanese uniform, because it was ruled that he had retained his U.S. citizenship. His actions amounted to war crimes, but because he was deemed an American, he could not also be a war criminal. As Justice Douglas wrote, "American citizenship until lost carries obligations of allegiance as well as privileges and benefits." For his cruelty above and beyond the call of Japanese duty, Mr. Kawakita was sentenced to death.

The Question of Voting

Thanks to another Japanese dual national who spent some time in his homeland, the courts ruled that voting in a foreign election is not expatriating for a dual national under certain circumstances *(Takehara v. Dulles)*. Initially the ruling was very limited (Mr. Takehara feared he would lose his ration card during the war and the Occupation). But civil libertarians have extended the ruling in subsequent cases.

Who is an Enemy?

By law, you may not commit treason or espionage against one of your nationalities because of loyalty to or coercion by the other, then later plead that your actions should be discounted. However, if you were required to perform normal military service or to vote, you can maintain your dual nationalities. You may be forced to.

In 1867, the United States was unable to prevent two naturalized citizens who had started an insurrection in Ireland from being tried for treason. Warren and Costello were sentenced to hang for treason to Britain.

Naturalized Americans who propagandize for their former country can denaturalized, according to a series of rulings by American courts in the cases of Germans and Nazis *(U.S. v. Kramer, 1919; Paul Krauer v. U.S.,* and *Schurman v. U.S.).* Naturalization is revoked, because it is presumed that the person took the oath of full faith and allegiance with some reserve. "The criterion of original fraud must be subsequent conduct," the court ruled.

Under international law, if a law pertains to enemy aliens, sequestration of foreign-owned property, war damages, or almost any other aspect of law, it applies to *all* people who hold that nationality, even if they also have another.

A country can determine who its enemies are. Hence, it was perfectly legal under U.S. and international law for Japanese who may have been dual nationals (as well as Japanese-Americans who had only U.S. citizenship) to be placed in camps during World War II. The decision to treat people as enemy aliens if they hold the second nationality of an enemy country has been tested and retested in both international and domestic courts and upheld. In Romania, you can be considered a German by right of birth and therefore subject to restrictions on trading with the enemy — even if you have succeeded to the Albanian throne, as was proven by Princess Sophia of Albania.

Chapter 5

Expatriation

J ust as you can gain nationality by various means, you also can lose it by many means. Most of us are concerned with U.S. nationality in particular. International lawyers agree that it is more difficult to retain U.S. citizenship if it was acquired by naturalization or by birth to U.S. parents in a foreign country than if it was acquired by birth in the United States. Naturalized persons are most vulnerable to losing their U.S. citizenship; foreign-born Americans by birth are slightly less vulnerable; and native-born Americans are almost untouchable. Dual nationals are always in greater danger of losing their American nationality.

You can lose your U.S. citizenship by specific legislated expatriating acts. *In some instances,* taking up a foreign nationality is an expatriating act for Americans.

Arbitrary Expatriation and International Law

In 1948, the Universal Declaration of Human Rights of the United Nations addressed the question of expatriation, but the declaration was not legally binding on U.N. member countries. Article 15 read, "No one shall be arbitrarily deprived of his nationality nor denied the right to change his nationality." ("His" under international law includes "her.")

Under national and international law, human rights notions have influenced rulings (although they are not formalized by treaty). One is that people may not be deprived of nationality by governments against their will. The language is incorporated in Article 15 of the U.N. Declaration on Human Rights. It has strongly influenced U.S. case law.

What is Expatriating?

Exercise of one nationality without renunciation of the other under international law does not amount to the renunciation of the other. U.S. law has followed this notion. *Mandoli v. Acheson* established in 1952 the legal principle that you cannot be expatriated by residence in the country of your dual or third nationality.

Under international law, you cannot be deprived of one nationality because of something imposed on you by the other you hold. And thanks to case law, being drafted cannot be expatriating for Americans — or Britishers or Canadians.

A principle of international law, based on the notion of comity (or good manners), says that a person who has two nationalities may not sue the country of one of his nationalities as if he were a citizen of the other. He must act in the same way as any other citizen of that country would be required to.

This was made a firm pillar of international jurisprudence by the U.S.-Egyptian Arbitral Tribunal in the Salem Case of 1932. "If two powers are both entitled by International Law to treat a person as their national, neither can raise a claim against the other in the name of such person."

This translates into a corollary, which basically says that if you (as a dual national) are sued in U.S. courts, you cannot defend yourself on the basis of having another nationality.

Problems arise because the country of origin refuses to recognize the legitimacy of the act of naturalization by a foreign power — and makes demands — most notably the draft. In the 1920s, France refused to give visas to French-born American nationals, claiming that they were still French citizens. Greece took away the American passports of Greek-born Americans and gave them Greek ones instead for their return journeys. This trend was followed by Yugoslavia and Turkey, which both decided to do the same.

The Soviet Union kept Aaron Gurvich and his wife Vera from leaving the country, even though they had been born in the United States and were U.S. citizens. It was only in 1935 that they were allowed to leave the Soviet Union (with no change in principle, but as a gesture of goodwill), thanks to the personal battle of then U.S. Ambassador George Kennan.

Naturalization By a Foreign Power

Even naturalization by a foreign power does not expatriate an American under certain circumstances, such as duress. An example is being an American woman in France who was married to a Frenchman and unable to flee France because of pregnancy when the Germans occupied the country. The lady in question took out a French nationality certificate to avoid a concentration camp. She successfully sued to be deemed not to have expatriated herself of her U.S. nationality *(Doreau v. Marshall)*. Once again, the courts have ruled against restrictive interpretation of the expatriation rules.

In effect, you cannot be expatriated even if you want to be — as long as you have not performed a specific expatriating act under U.S. law (and even if you have, if you are prepared to sue and you have a good lawyer). U.S. rulings are continually whittling down the number of acts that are considered expatriating. The same thing is taking place in other countries as well, thanks to a greater respect for civil liberties worldwide.

Naturalization and Expatriation

The United States and Britain remained aloof from the trend toward adopting the Napoleonic Code and getting into the business of defining nationality, to their detriment. They left it to *jus soli* — which meant that they were unsure what to do with immigrants.

It took the great English jurist Coke many chapters to argue that people born in Scotland after the Act of Union between England and Scotland (the ascension of James I/VI) would have standing in a court of law in England, and vice versa. It was only in 1707 that a Scot was defined as a non-alien in England. This is a sign of the narrow localism of the Anglo-Saxon Common Law, from which American nationality law stems.

Immigrants were granted U.S. nationality as far as the colonies were concerned, and as far as the United States was concerned after 1790, but Britain continued to treat all those who emigrated from Britain as if they remained British citizens. This led to the last war between the two English-speaking countries, the War of 1812, whose *casus belli* was the "impressment" by the British Navy of American sailors. Because Britain did not recognize their naturalization as Americans, they were still subject to the British naval draft. It was not possible in British eyes to renounce British nationality, or, to quote the judges, *"nemo potest exuere patriam."*

It is worth noting that the United States, despite having fought the War of 1812 and including naturalization as a principle in the Constitution, agreed with this principle. Until 1868, it was impossible under U.S. law to renounce U.S. nationality either.

Expatriating Acts for Americans

You can no longer lose your U.S. citizenship for moving back to your country of origin. You can no longer lose it for marrying a Hindu or a Chinese. You can no longer lose it for becoming a Communist or a Nazi after your naturalization; although you still can lose it if you were a Communist or a Nazi and swore a false oath of loyalty to the U.S. Constitution at the moment of your naturalization, and this is not considered a violation of the Bill of Rights.

You probably will have difficulty getting American citizenship if you are an adult foreigner guilty of "moral turpitude" (the words of the law) or who otherwise is unappealing to the U.S. government: because of a criminal record, because of Communist Party membership, because you can be accused of being a terrorist, because of sexual orientation (including practicing prostitution or homosexuality), or because of ill health. Some of these restrictions are being tested in the courts.

But you cannot lose your U.S. citizenship once acquired because of a subsequent change in your sexual orientation or

health, or because you become a criminal in America.
(Although, in the 1950s, naturalized Americans who had joined
the Communist Party were stripped of their nationality and
deported.) You can lose your American citizenship by
naturalization if you lied about one of these conditions on the
application, because then the naturalization is deemed to have
been procured by fraud. This is the basis on which the U.S.
revokes citizenship and deports those accused of being Nazi
war criminals decades after they obtained American citizenship.

You cannot lose U.S. citizenship, however acquired, if you
are given nationality by a foreign country through no fault of
your own, or if you are drafted by a foreign country. You can
only lose it if a foreign country gives you its citizenship upon
your own naturalization. However, such expatriation via
naturalization specifically excludes actions such as pointing out
to the foreign government circumstances that automatically
grant you the right to that nationality. Sending the government
a copy of your grandmother's birth certificate is not an
expatriating act. In fact, despite the way immigration lawyers
explain the situation, it is difficult today to lose your U.S.
citizenship. (Although any naturalized American, as opposed to
a citizen by birth, should be much more cautious.)

Any act performed under duress (including being drafted by
a foreign country) is not expatriating.

Expatriating acts today include: naturalization in a foreign
state upon your own application *with the intent to lose U.S.
citizenship*; taking an oath of allegiance or the equivalent to a
foreign country *with the intent to lose U.S. citizenship*;
unauthorized service in foreign armed forces; or making a
formal renunciation in the form suggested by the Department of
State.

The Supreme Court (in the matter of Harrison) ruled that
foreign military service cannot be held against an immigrant in

the course of filling the five years' residence requirement — so you can be considered a U.S. resident while serving in a foreign army against your will for as long as 3¼ years. A series of cases involving American-Jewish men, who went to Israel, were granted Israeli nationality, and drafted, has essentially removed the penalty of loss of nationality for those drafted abroad. If you plan to serve in a foreign army, you should write a declaration to the U.S. Embassy in that country stating that you do not wish this to be treated as an expatriating act. While such a letter by itself has no legal standing, it can be an element of proof should you have to prove that you did not intend to relinquish U.S. citizenship.

There also have been cases, for example, of Franco-American dual nationals who chose to attend the Ecole Polytechnique, an elite French engineering school whose graduates are required to serve as military officers to pay for their free tuition and room and board, who made such a declaration and were not deemed to have lost their U.S. nationality. You should seek legal advice before undertaking this kind of act.

British Expatriates

The situation in Britain, however, is very different; becoming a tax exile is common, and many pop stars of disc and screen maintain foreign domiciles to avoid British income taxes entirely. They do not have to give up British nationality. In Britain, as in most of the world, you are not required to pay taxes to your country of citizenship, but only to your country of residence. Apart from the United States, the only country that taxes its citizens wherever they may live is the Philippines, because the U.S. Internal Revenue Code became the tax law of the Philippines in 1946 when they became independent from the United States.

In 1870, which was rather a long time after the War of 1812 but only two years after the United States abandoned the notion of *nemo potest exuere patriam,* Britain finally yielded and allowed people who were becoming naturalized British citizens to renounce their former nationalities. But it was not required. It still is not required.

Britain instituted a system of almost pure *jus soli.* And then with the enactment of laws in 1911, 1914, 1915, and 1922, the country went completely the other way, adopting a system of *jus sanguinis.* The initial reason, ironically, given the Falklands War, was to allow the huge British colony in Argentina to continue to owe tribute to His Majesty.

In 1911, the British nationality law heralded the concept of Empire with the Imperial Conference, covering the white Commonwealth countries (Britain, Canada, Australia, New Zealand, and initially Newfoundland and South Africa). These lands recognized each other's right to interchange nationality. The key word was that you had to be born within His Majesty's allegiance to a father who also had been born within that allegiance. In other words, you had to have essentially British genes. The Empire then proved its loyalty by sending many volunteers to England during the 1914-1918 war.

However, most of the territories of His Majesty's allegiance have grown up a bit since 1911 and in the 1930s specifically ruled out commonwealth reciprocity. Some Commonwealth countries, such as Britain, Australia, Jamaica, and Belize, still do not require that you renounce your former nationality upon acquiring theirs.

Under the British law passed in 1922, offspring of a British parent (originally a British father, but changed in 1948 to include mothers as well) are British even if they have a second nationality, *of one of His Majesty's dominions.* (It is this last phrase that leaves out most Americans of British ancestry.) As a result, many Australians, South Africans, and New Zealanders also have British nationality. A more general result of this tradition is that accepting a foreign nationality is not an expatriating act in Britain.

The trouble is that most Americans of British stock cannot benefit from the 1922 law, because their ancestors some generations back renounced British nationality upon becoming American, and the intervening generations failed to register with the British Embassy the birth of children born after 1915. Anyone whose British male ancestor became American after 1906, you will recall, is descended from a Briton who had had to expatriate himself when he became American. Ditto for someone whose ex-British female ancestor became American after 1922. However, if you have a British parent who did not become an American citizen, you may find that you can apply for British nationality.

A large number of British war-brides kept their British nationality or have a right to reassume it today. The offspring of the baby-boom generation whose mothers were or are British can apply for British citizenship and passports all these years later, and have a good chance of getting them. If your mother or grandmother was a war-bride, you have a relatively short genealogy to prove.

Recently, the right to be British was retroactively taken away from some who had held it previously, notably Chinese from Hong Kong and people of Indian background from East Africa. The fact that their fathers and/or mothers had been born within His Majesty's allegiance ceased to be the determining factor, because they were the wrong color. (Remember the old U.S. laws against Asians before you become too righteous about this.) Under the racially-inspired changes in British laws, a special class of passports for subjects of the Queen was invented that does not give you the right to live and work in

Britain or to transmit nationality to your children. Such passports are the only ones given to people born outside the United Kingdom in territories that became British by annexation. That was the legal dodge.

Another restriction denied the right to acquire British nationality to persons born wholly outside British lands to parents who were not British — if either their fathers or mothers were also naturalized outside the United Kingdom or not British at all. Intended to trap members of other races, it also occasionally harms naturalized white Britons. If your war-bride parent or grandmother married a black or Asian American, be prepared to face uncooperative British consuls.

The British have now created five classes of citizenship. All are entitled to British-type passports, but only the first class is permitted to live and work in Britain. Members of the first category are called "British citizens;" the lesser classes are "British dependent territories citizens," "British overseas citizens," "British subjects," and "British protected persons." What makes it all more confusing is that until the latest Nationality Act, all Britishers legally were called "British subjects."

Expatriates of Other Nationalities

Some countries, notably Japan and China, in theory impose loss of their nationalities of origin on all those who become citizens, not only by naturalization, but also by birth. In practice, anyone born in Japan can become Japanese only if he is without another nationality. The Japanese have managed to avoid giving Japanese nationality to Koreans born in Japan — even those born to Korean parents who can claim many generations of residence in Japan.

Here's how they do it. Japanese nationality is given to any child born in Japan to a Japanese mother if the child's father is unknown; it is also given to a child born in Japan to a Japanese mother if the father has no nationality. A child born in Japan whose parents are unknown and who would have no other nationality also automatically becomes Japanese. A child of a Japanese father becomes Japanese at birth wherever it is born. Thus the only way for a pure Korean child born in Japan to be granted Japanese nationality would be if it were an abandoned foundling.

The United States insists that any naturalized citizen give up any prior nationality. The idea that you have to give up your former nationality to adopt a new one was also adopted by France, Italy, Mexico, Spain, and Portugal, but they are less stringent about imposing the restriction than the United States. As already noted, Britain specifically does not make this requirement; nor do most former British territories. In practice, the situation is much more lax even in the south of Europe than the law would lead you to believe.

Italy gives its nationality to a child born on its soil on condition it lives in Italy, even if its parents are both not Italian; the result is to create infant dual nationals. Italy also gives citizenship to the spouse of an Italian after six months if the couple lives in Italy or after three years if the couple lives abroad, a rule that can be particularly useful for Italian-American families and those marrying into them.

Spain and Portugal legally give instant citizenship to a child born on their territory, who of course may have another nationality or two because of its parents. Marrying a Spaniard gets you a passport with a one-year wait; marrying a Portuguese gets you an immediate passport. None of these countries will check with the authorities of other countries to see if any also have granted citizenship to the same spouse or child. The reason is that authorities in these countries refuse to operate in any language but their own. So they cannot possibly write letters or telexes to the authorities in the United States (whose mastery of foreign languages is similarly great) describing the issue of a passport to Niño Smith or Sposa Menotti or John Philip Sousa.

If you know anything at all about France, you will realize that the same linguistic barrier protects you there, too.

French nationality can be adopted by people who have another nationality. The most common case involves the offspring of immigrants to France from countries such as Algeria and Portugal; they are allowed to serve in one army (all three countries have the draft) while maintaining their nationality in the other.

In practice, the French allow you to become French and keep a foreign nationality when you marry a French citizen and stay with him or her for at least six months. In practice (although not by law), the French grant French nationality to children of mixed marriages in which one parent is French. They also grant nationality to any baby born in France. Again, this is not a law, it is a practice. The point is that, by law, being born in France does not give you a French passport. But in practice it does. Just as, by law, being born in Britain does not give you a British passport. But in practice it does. And no one asks your baby to give up any prior nationality.

The countries that legally give nationality to any baby born on their territory (with the exceptions, at least in theory, of diplomatic infants and those born to occupying forces) include: the United States, Argentina, Australia, Austria, Barbados, Belize, Bolivia, Brazil, Canada, Chile, Costa Rica, the Dominican Republic, Ecuador, Greece, Honduras, Ireland, Israel, Italy (with a residence requirement), Jamaica, Lebanon, Malta, Mauritius, Mexico, New Zealand, Panama, Paraguay, Portugal,

Spain, St. Kitts, Thailand, Trinidad, Turkey, Uruguay, and Venezuela.

It is interesting to note that Mexico and Britain consider their ships and airplanes to be national territory and issue birth certificates that can be converted to passports to babies of whatever nationality born on their vessels (including airplanes).

Chapter 6
Dual Nationality Under U.S. Law

T he Supreme Court of the United States has stated that dual nationality is "a status long recognized in the law" and that "a person may have and exercise rights of nationality in two countries and be subject to the responsibilities of both. The mere fact that he asserts the rights of one citizenship does not without more mean that he renounces the other," *Kawakita v. U.S., 343 U.S. 717 (1952).*

Dual nationality results from the fact that there is no uniform rule of international law relating to the acquisition of nationality. Each country has its own laws on the subject, and its nationality is conferred upon individuals on the basis of its own domestic policy. Individuals may have dual nationality not by choice but by automatic operation of these different and sometimes conflicting laws.

The laws of the United States, no less than those of other countries, contribute to the situation because they provide for acquisition of U.S. citizenship by birth in the United States and also by birth abroad to an American, regardless of the other nationalities which a person might acquire at birth. For example, a child born abroad to U.S. citizens may acquire at birth not only American citizenship but also the nationality of the country in which it was born. Similarly, a child born in the United States to foreigners may acquire at birth both U.S. citizenship and a foreign nationality.

The laws of some countries provide for automatic acquisition of citizenship after birth, for example, by marriage. In addition, some countries do not recognize naturalization in a foreign state as grounds for loss of citizenship. A person from one of those countries who is naturalized in the United States keeps the nationality of the country of origin despite the fact that one of the requirements for U.S. naturalization is a renunciation of other nationalities.

The current nationality laws of the United States do not specifically refer to dual nationality.

The automatic acquisition or retention of a foreign nationality does not affect U.S. citizenship; however, the acquisition of a foreign nationality upon one's own application or the application of a duly authorized agent may cause loss of U.S. citizenship under Section 349(a)(1) of the Immigration and Nationality Act [8 U.S.C. 1481(a)(1)].

In order for loss of nationality to occur under Section 349(a)(1), it must be established that the naturalization was obtained voluntarily by a person 18 years of age or older with the intention of relinquishing U.S. citizenship. Such an intention may be shown by the person's statements or conduct, *Vance v. Terrazas, 444 U.S. 252 (1980)*. If the U.S. government is unable to prove that the person had such an intention when applying for and obtaining the foreign citizenship, the person will have both nationalities.

United States law does not contain any provisions requiring U.S. citizens who are born with dual nationality to choose one nationality or the other when they become adults. It is a popular misconception that the law requires such a choice to be made.

Section 215 of the Immigration and Nationality Act (8 U.S.C. 1185) requires U.S. citizens to use U.S. passports when entering or leaving the United States unless one of the exceptions listed in Section 53.2 of Title 22 of the Code of Federal Regulations applies. Dual nationals may be required by the other country of which they are citizens to enter and leave that country using its passport, but they do not endanger their U.S. citizenship by complying with such a requirement.

Most (but not all) countries have laws which specify how a citizen may lose or divest citizenship. Generally, persons who do not wish to maintain dual nationality may renounce the citizenship which they do not want. Americans may renounce their U.S. citizenship abroad pursuant to Section 349(a)(5) of the Immigration and Nationality Act [(8 U.S.C. 1481(a)(5)].

Chapter 7
Formal Renunciation Of U.S. Citizenship

U nited States citizens have the right to remain citizens until they intend to give up citizenship. It is also the right of every citizen to relinquish United States citizenship. Section 349(a) of the Immigration and Nationality Act (8 U.S.C. 1481) states:

a person who is a national of the United States whether by birth or naturalization, shall lose his nationality by voluntarily performing any of the following acts with the intention of relinquishing United States nationality:...

(5) making a formal renunciation of nationality before a diplomatic or consular officer of the United States in a foreign state, in such form as may be prescribed by the Secretary of State; or

(6) making in the United States a formal written renunciation of nationality in such form as may be prescribed by, and before such officer as may be designated by, the Attorney General, whenever the United States shall be in a state of war and the Attorney General shall approve such renunciation as not contrary to the interests of national defense...

Renunciation is the most unequivocal way in which a person can manifest an intention to relinquish U.S. citizenship. In order for a renunciation under Section 349(a)(5) to be effective, all of the conditions of the statute must be met. In other words, a person wishing to renounce American citizenship must appear in person and sign an oath of renunciation before a U.S. consular or diplomatic officer abroad, generally at an American Embassy or Consulate. Renunciations which are not in the form prescribed by the Secretary of State have no legal effect. Because of the way in which Section 349(a)(5) is written and interpreted, Americans cannot effectively renounce their citizenship by mail, through an agent, or while in the United States.

Section 349(a)(6) provides for renunciation of United States citizenship under certain circumstances in the United States when the United States is in a state of war.

Once a renunciation is done before an American diplomatic or consular officer abroad, all documents are referred to the Department of State. The Director of the Office of Overseas Citizens Services reviews them to ensure all the criteria under the act have been met. It is not true that the renunciation can be refused on a discretionary basis — the right to renounce is absolute.

Parents cannot renounce United States citizenship on behalf of their children. Before an oath of renunciation will be administered under Section 349(a)(5), persons under the age of 18 must convince a U.S. diplomatic or consular officer that they fully understand the nature and consequences of the oath of renunciation and are voluntarily seeking to renounce their citizenship. United States common law establishes an arbitrary limit of age 14 under which a child's understanding must be established by substantial evidence.

Under Section 351(b) of the Immigration and Nationality Act [8 U.S.C. 1483(b)], a person who renounced U.S. citizenship before the age of 18 years and "who within six months after attaining the age of eighteen years asserts his claim to United States nationality in such manner as the Secretary of State shall by regulation prescribe, shall not be deemed to have expatriated himself..." The relevant regulation is Section 50.20(b) of Title 22 of the Code of Federal Regulations which requires that the person take an oath of allegiance to the United States before a diplomatic or consular officer in order to retain U.S. citizenship.

Persons who contemplate renunciation of U.S. nationality should be aware that, unless they already possess a foreign nationality or are assured of acquiring another nationality shortly after completing their renunciation, severe hardship could result. In the absence of a second nationality, those individuals would become stateless. As stateless persons, they would not be entitled to the protection of any government. They might also find it difficult or impossible to travel, as they would probably not be entitled to a passport from any country. Further, a person who has renounced U.S. nationality will be required to apply for a visa to travel to the United States, just as other aliens do. If found ineligible for a visa, a renunciant could be permanently barred from the United States. Renunciation of American citizenship does not necessarily prevent a former citizen's deportation from a foreign country to the United States.

Persons considering renunciation should also be aware that the fact that they have renounced U.S. nationality may have no effect whatsoever on their U.S. tax or military service obligations. Nor will it allow them to escape possible prosecution for crimes which they may have committed in the

United States, or repayment of financial obligations previously incurred in the United States.

Finally, those contemplating a renunciation of U.S. citizenship should understand that renunciation is irrevocable, except as provided in Section 351 of the Immigration and Nationality Act, and cannot be canceled or set aside without successful administrative or judicial appeal (which is wildly unlikely).

Chapter 8
American Tax Exiles

The $70,000 — and More —
Offshore Loophole for U.S. Citizens

I f you're a typical cash-poor American, you could increase your standard of living dramatically if you could avoid throwing away 40% or more of your income on taxes each year. Thousands of Americans are doing that right now, and many more can. It's one of the clearest provisions in the tax code.

The loophole is known as the foreign-earned-income-exclusion. It allows for U.S. citizens who live and work outside the U.S. to exclude from gross income up to $70,000 of foreign-earned income. In addition, an employer-provided housing allowance can be excluded from income. There are other tax breaks available: Each member of a married couple working overseas, for example, can exclude salary of up to $70,000. That's a total of $140,000, *plus* housing allowances.

It is important to note that this is not a deduction, credit, or deferral. *It is an outright exclusion of the income from gross income.*

Naturally, to get these benefits you have to meet certain requirements:

- You must establish a tax home in a foreign country.
- You must pass either the "foreign-residence test" or the "physical-presence test."
- You must have earned income.

In the IRS view of the world, your tax home is the location of your regular or principal place of business. That is, the tax home is where you work, not where you live.

But the definition goes further for the foreign-earned-income exclusion. This is a trap that catches many Americans overseas who think they are earning tax free income. If you work overseas and maintain a place of residence in the United States, your tax home is not outside the U.S. In other words, to qualify for the foreign-earned-income exclusion you have to establish both your principal place of business and your residence outside the United States.

This trap catches a number of construction and oil workers. These workers generally work on a construction site or oil platform for three to six months. They get a few weeks or months off. Many of them make the mistake of leaving their family and personal possessions at their U.S. home and visiting this home during their vacations. They can't use the offshore loophole because they never establish a tax home outside the United States. They maintained a place of residence in the United States. *You need to sell or rent your U.S. home and establish a primary residence outside the United States.*

After establishing your tax home, you must pass one of two additional tests.

Counting the Days

The more straightforward test is the physical presence test. To pass the test, you must be outside of the United States for 330 days out of any 12 consecutive months. The days, of course, do not have to be consecutive. That sounds very simple, but there are a number of smaller rules that can complicate it. Few people begin their foreign assignments on January 1st and end them on December 31st. Thus for most people, the first and last 12 months of their overseas stay will occupy two tax years. This requires them to prorate their income and the $70,000 exclusion for those tax years.

In addition, to count a day as one spent outside of the United States, you must be out of the United States for the entire day. There are exceptions for traveling days and days spent flying over the United States if the flight did not originate there. The IRS has a number of rules on counting days.

If you are going to travel back and forth between the United States and foreign countries and if you want to try to pass this test, you'll have to learn the rules and count days very carefully.

The subjective test, known as the foreign-residence test, is probably easier for most taxpayers to pass. You must establish yourself as a bona fide resident of a foreign country or countries for an uninterrupted period that includes an entire taxable year, and you must intend to stay there indefinitely. If you do not pass this test, you are considered by the IRS a transient, or sojourner, instead of a foreign resident, and will not qualify as a foreign resident.

According to the tax law, your residence is a state of mind. It is where you intend to be domiciled indefinitely. To determine your state of mind, the IRS looks at the degree of your attachment to the country in question. A number of factors, none of them decisive or significantly more important than the others, are examined. The bottom line is that you establish yourself as a member of a foreign community. Certainly having dual nationality and residing in your other country of citizenship is an extremely helpful factor in establishing this proof of residence for the IRS.

Which Income to Exclude

Once you have qualified for the offshore loophole, you must identify the kind of income that qualifies. *Not all income qualifies for the exclusion — only foreign-earned income.*

Foreign-earned income is income paid for services you have performed in a foreign country. This includes salaries, professional fees, tips, and similar compensation. Interest, dividends, and capital gains do not qualify.

Self-employed people must adhere to some additional rules. Professionals who do not make material use of capital in performing their services can qualify all of their net income for the loophole. But when both personal services and capital are used to generate income, no more than 30% of net profits will be considered eligible for the exclusion. Note that for self-employed individuals and for partners, the *net income* is the amount that is applied toward the exclusion limit, not the gross income.

The $70,000 limit on the offshore loophole applies to individual taxpayers. So if you are married, you and your spouse potentially can exclude up to $140,000 of foreign-earned income. But you cannot share each other's limit. For example, if one of you earns $80,000 and the other earns $30,000, you exclude only $100,000 on the return ($70,000 plus $30,000).

Don't Close the Loophole

Too many U.S. expatriates inadvertently close the offshore loophole. There are several ways of doing this.

One way is not to realize that the provision has requirements that must be met. Many Americans assume that since they are living overseas, everything they do is free from U.S. tax. That's not so. It is well worth your while to discuss the matter with a tax attorney or accountant who understands the offshore loophole. Go over your situation and your plans in detail *before* leaving the United States. That way, you'll be sure to qualify for, and make maximum use of, this loophole.

Another way people close this loophole is by not filing tax returns. To get the exemption, *you must file a tax return and claim the exemption on Form 2555.* The IRS has had success in recent years contending that anyone who does not file the return loses the loophole, even if he meets all the requirements. Be sure you file the return and properly claim the loophole. The loophole exempts your foreign-earned income from tax, but it does not exempt you from the filing requirement.

Recent tax laws, plus some heavy criticism from the General Accounting Office, have caused the IRS to increase its monitoring of U.S. citizens overseas. The IRS now reviews passport applications and renewals to ensure that you not receive or renew a passport unless your tax returns are filed and paid up. The IRS is also looking for expatriate Americans and informing them of their tax obligations. It is estimated that about two-thirds of expatriate Americans are not filing any U.S. tax returns, and the IRS aims to change that. Be sure to file your tax returns.

Taxes and Renunciation of U.S. Citizenship

Once your citizenship is renounced, you are subject to the same tax rules as a foreigner, or alien. If you are a non-resident alien, which means you are not in the United States for more than 183 days during the year, you are taxed in the United States only on income from U.S. sources. This includes rents, royalties, interest, dividends, and capital gains from U.S. real property; interest dispositions, salaries, and self-employment income earned in the United States, and other items. If you reside in a country that has a tax treaty with the United States, the withholding taxes on the U.S.-source investment income could be 20% or less.

If you reside in the United States for more than 183 days (six months) during the year, you are considered a resident alien. This means that you are taxed in the United States on your worldwide income, just as citizens are, though you renounce your citizenship. So there is no tax advantage to renouncing citizenship, unless you plan to permanently move your residence outside the United States.

But the tax code gives the United States the right to continue taxing your U.S.-source income for 10 years if the IRS decides that one of the principal aims of the renunciation is the avoidance of U.S. taxes. The IRS is likely to exercise this right when you sell U.S. assets and reap large capital gains. Beyond this, it is not clear why the IRS chooses to ignore or to scrutinize the renunciation of citizenship, nor is it clear how its review process works.

One of the best sources of information on this topic is *The Tax Exile Report* by the American lawyer and tax expert, Marshall J. Langer. His book discusses the laws — including residence, domicile, and citizenship — for tax exiles from many countries, including the U.S., Britain, France, Canada, Germany, and the Nordic countries. *The Tax Exile Report* is published by Scope International Ltd. (Forestside House, Forestside, Rowlands Castle, Hants., PO9 6EE, Great Britain), who will send a free catalog on request.

Acquiring a Second Nationality as Part of Asset Protection Planning

One of the unhappy facts of financial life in our lawsuit-happy society is the increasing danger of being sued. And if you should have the misfortune to wind up on the receiving end of some courtroom debacle, it could easily cost you your life savings.

One of the best ways to protect yourself against such a calamity is to have professionals prepare an asset protection plan in advance of any problems.

Doing so is not expensive, and provides a great deal of assurance that you and your family will have the benefit of the money you have built up through years of work. Asset protection plans are a relatively new area of law, prepared by lawyers who specialize in protecting what you own instead of suing people.

Asset protection is different from traditional retirement or estate planning. It is the systematic and integrated protection of your family and business from risk. Most financial planning is intended to help you establish wealth so you can retire, and pass on as much of that wealth as possible to your family after death.

Asset protection plans include estate plans but are intended to also help you keep your wealth while you are living. They often involve legal structures such as family limited partnerships, children's trusts, exempt assets, offshore trust arrangements and living trusts.

Asset protection offers you an advantage over other approaches to financial planning. For example, more lawsuits are being filed today than at any time in history. Statistics indicate that the average American faces a greater risk of being in court than in the hospital. Other situations include bankruptcy filings, taxation, insurance company failures or bank financing.

With an increasing number of government forfeitures of property and IRS seizures, in addition to civil lawsuits, asset protection strategies become an important part of advance planning.

Although many people become involved in asset protection strategies such as offshore trusts, family limited partnerships, and non-seizable foreign annuities, few concern themselves with adding personal protection to the package.

Yet, by having a second nationality in reserve, in truly desperate circumstances a person has the option to leave U.S. jurisdiction and renounce U.S. citizenship, an option that would not exist without having the other citizenship already in place.

Asset protection plans are fully legal. It is not something for people who might want to avoid the law or their other responsibilities. The law is clear as to what is permissible and what is not. Asset protection simply gives protection against unfair lawsuits and gives a level playing field to operate from.

The goal is to structure the plan so you never have to misrepresent yourself or worry about the legality of the plan.

The best way to do this is to seek the assistance of professionals, and there is now a firm that works with clients from all over the country. They can also work with your existing lawyers or accountants if you wish. As part of the overall planning and investment process, they can often arrange that some of the investments be made in jurisdictions that will confer a citizenship, thus providing an additional benefit while also gaining protection of the assets. Because the planning process tends to document the credentials and credibility of the applicant, it is sometimes possible to obtain citizenship of a major country that would not ordinarily make citizenship available. For information on asset protection planning services write: Asset Protection Corporation, Suite 201A, 14418 Old Mill Road, Upper Marlboro, MD 20772.

The "Option Strategy" for Tax Planning

Many publications talk about the value of offshore techniques to defer taxes. Creation of an offshore business will generally defer taxation until dividends are paid, allowing untaxed profits to compound in the foreign corporation. Purchase of an annuity from Switzerland allows deferral of the tax until payments from the annuity begin to be made.

But this is as far as most publications take the subject, and that is missing one of the great values of such investments. Tax-deferral creates an option to become tax-free in the future, a decision which may never be taken — but the option on the decision costs nothing. At any point in the future, if an American citizen decides to expatriate himself by renouncing his U.S. citizenship, the accumulated profits of the business or the annuity can be withdrawn totally tax-free. Tax-deferral automatically becomes tax avoidance once the U.S. citizenship is gone.

This "option strategy" also works for inheritance taxes. With proper tax planning, one can create a large estate, and if one renounces U.S. citizenship shortly before death, that entire estate can pass tax-free to one's heirs. Thus a person is able to maintain and use their U.S. citizenship throughout their lifetime, and then take the option of renunciation of citizenship

when citizenship is no longer relevant — perhaps when living
in an overseas retirement haven.

Chapter 9
Refugees

Swedish Nationality for American Draft Evaders and Deserters

Many Americans who opposed the Vietnam War (including deserters) found their way to Sweden. The Swedes have a seven-year residence requirement, but they maintain only very slight elements of *jus sanguinis* in their legal system. So it is relatively easy if you live there to become a Swede. There is no explicit rule against dual nationality, but the neo-Swede theoretically must prove that he has the consent of his first nationality upon becoming Swedish; in practice, this was not an obstacle to American draft-evaders and deserters, who were perfectly willing to renounce their U.S. citizenship. Once you have become a Swede, however, you lose your citizenship if you apply for a foreign nationality — including re-applying for U.S. citizenship under the draft amnesty.

Because of the rule stipulating that your prior nationality must agree to your becoming Swedish, it is difficult to acquire Swedish nationality by marrying a Swede.

Spanish Jews

For reasons that remain obscure, Generalissimo Franco offered Spanish passports to Jews during World War II. The rationale was that their ancestors had been expelled from Spain unjustly in 1492 by the Inquisition, but individuals were not required to provide genealogical evidence. There are many theories why Franco, who gained power in Spain thanks to help from Hitler and Mussolini, deliberately undermined the Nazi policy of rounding up and deporting Jews. One theory is that Franco was of Jewish ancestry himself; another theory is that he wanted to be sure to survive the collapse of the Axis.

Today, Spanish nationality is not given wholesale. However, persons of Sephardic background can become Spanish with a shorter residence requirement (one year) than others (who must wait 10 years). Sephardic is the Hebrew term for Jews of Spanish descent who pronounce Hebrew according to their own rules, and who use certain distinctive melodies in their synagogues. It is helpful if you speak the language of the East European Sephardic, called Ladino, which is quite close to classic Spanish although it is written with Hebrew letters. Having a distinctly Spanish name also helps. The matter is handled on a case-by-case basis. Others of Spanish background, including South Americans, Filipinos, and Puerto Ricans, also can acquire Spanish nationality on an accelerated basis. Actually, Spain has dual nationality agreements with most Spanish-American countries. Citizens of these countries can gain entry into Spain without visas — for the moment. Because of the arrival of members of Colombian drug cartels, Spain is under strong pressure from the EU to stop giving preference to persons from Latin America. But several years of such pressure have not changed the law, and Spain is very concerned with its traditional ties to Latin America.

Under Spanish law, acquiring Spanish nationality requires that you renounce any prior nationality; in practice, it does not.

Political Refugees in Other Countries

Children born in Britain to German-Jewish refugees from Nazi Germany became British with full rights. Many of their fathers, however, were held on the Isle of Man for the duration of the war or until they signed up for the service, to separate the Jews from the Nazis (which was not always easy for the British to do, because they refused to listen to anybody with a German accent who sought to advise them). A few very prominent refugees who were so well-know to the British as to be beyond reproach were quietly able to avoid internment on the Isle of Man.

Children born outside Britain to refugees who subsequently became British are not fully British under the current Nationality Act, and they are therefore not automatically allowed to live and work in Britain. If they also have a right to German nationality, many of them are claiming it. This then allows them to use EU preference to avoid British obstacles. The irony here is evidently lost on the British.

Similarly, ethnic Chinese from the British colony of Hong Kong, which will be absorbed by Communist China in 1997, are desperate to obtain foreign nationality; Britain has indicated it will not allow them to live and work in Britain on the basis of their British dependency (Hong Kong) passports. About

100,000 have been taken in by Macao, which belongs to Portugal. But Macao will be returned to China shortly after Hong Kong is returned. These Chinese can get Portuguese nationality in six years, and Portuguese travel documents even sooner. They then can travel freely within the EU and go to work in England. Again, the irony seems lost on the British.

Political refugees are issued papers more quickly and have an edge during the nationalization process in many countries, including Canada, Germany, Austria, Switzerland and Italy. But with recent widespread abuses by "economic" rather than "political" refugees, this is becoming more difficult. And almost impossible for an American, with no Vietnam war to be fleeing from.

Africa is Not for Afro-Americans

Many Africans want to adopt another nationality for economic-political reasons. Within Africa, they are usually made unwelcome by neighboring states. Many work illegally across the border in relatively more prosperous countries, such as Nigeria, Senegal, and the Ivory Coast — but they are not allowed to acquire those nationalities. Persons of the approved religion (Moslem or Christian, depending on the country) or whose tribes straddle the frontier have an easier time changing African citizenship. American blacks are generally not welcomed by African authorities.

African refugees also tend to be made unwelcome even in countries where they have historic ties, such as Britain or France. The effect has been to create *de facto* racial tests in these countries. (The French consider persons from Martinique and Guadeloupe to be French citizens because those islands are legally part of France, just as Hawaii is part of the U.S.; a dream of many French-speaking Haitians is to pass for French West Indians.)

The only example of total acceptance of African refugees is the Israeli airlift and naturalization (upon landing) of so-called Falashas, or Ethiopian Jews; it did not work for Moslems, Christians, or animists. And even in the case of the Falashas, it took a battle with the rabbinical authorities to get those people's Jewish religious affiliation recognized.

Africans, West Indians, and Afro-Americans who want second passports are probably better off looking into countries in this hemisphere. St. Kitts and Nevis, Jamaica, and Belize, amongst others, grant their citizenships without requiring renunciation of former nationality.

Chapter 10
Stateless Papers
And No Papers

One of the pieces of bad advice that seems to float around the world of second passports is to become stateless and obtain stateless persons' travel documents. DON'T DO IT. A stateless person has no right to live and work anywhere, and despite international treaties on the issuance of stateless persons' travel documents, they are often not available at all.

Don't Buy a World Passport

In 1948, an American Quaker idealist named Garry Davis renounced his U.S. nationality in favor of World Citizenship and drove governments to frenzy (in fact to the point of jailing him) by flashing his World Citizenship passport around Europe. Davis has created something now called the World Service Authority (WSA), which issues travel documents to anyone by mail.

The WSA document is intended to serve as proof of identity without government involvement. The information on it regarding one's vital statistics, such as date of birth, must be sworn before a notary — thus, this is not a way to drink before you're of age.

The document is printed in the official U.N. languages (English, French, Spanish, Arabic, Russian, and Chinese, plus Esperanto). Although the official part of the document is printed in seven languages, the information about the person using the passport is written in the Roman alphabet.

In 1977, Davis tried to enter the United States with his World Citizenship passport and was stopped at the border. The INS said he needed a visa and refused to stamp one in his document. Davis sued and lost (*Davis v. U.S., Civ A. No. 79-1974*).

Six countries allegedly formally and officially recognize the WSA travel document as sufficient for entry and departure from their countries: Burkina Fasso, Ecuador, Mauritius, Togo, Yemen, and Zambia. A written inquiry to the appropriate authorities in each of these countries asking them to confirm this information and indicate their visa requirements for World Passport holders elicited no responses. In practice, followers of the world citizenship movement in the past 34 years have managed to gain visas and entry into more than 100 countries. Lives have been saved with this official-looking document in countries where the visa authorities cannot read, or cannot read any of the languages of the document, or can read (for example) the Arabic (official) part of the passport and not the bit where the holder's name is given as Moses Cohen. But it should be clearly understood that these admissions and visa stamps would generally be considered mistakes by the countries concerned, not a recognition of the passport.

The World Passport is an intriguing document, but it can be very dangerous if you believe in it and suddenly find yourself in jail in some obnoxious country that decides you are a spy. And since you did not enter that country on a recognized national passport you *do not* have the right to call the consulate of the U.S. or whatever other country you are claiming citizenship of. You are stuck with your initial declaration — you can't suddenly say, "I'm American, please call my consulate." Legally it is no different than any self-printed passport.

If you have a sense of adventure, and don't particularly care whether you are ever heard from again or not, feel free to try it. Or if you do survive your incarceration and torture in some dismal jail, write and tell us about it for some future edition of this book.

If you want one just for fun, or to use in some safer way than as your travel document, contact the World Service Authority, 1012 14th St. N.W., Suite 1101, Washington, DC 20005; (202) 638-2662. A three-year travel document costs $35, an eight-year one $60. In case you were wondering, it is not tax-deductible.

Chapter 11
A Word About Extradition

This book was written for those who have legitimate uses for a second nationality. In spite of this, some readers doubtless have in mind acquiring a second nationality with the thought of fleeing from some criminal warrant. Of course what is criminal is open to interpretation, as many refugees are "criminals" in the countries they fled from, but are granted political asylum by their destination country. Even Robert Vesco was granted political asylum by Cuba.

Although the United States has extradition treaties with most countries, actual extradition is rare. Governments cheat too. The United States Supreme Court has recently held that it is legal, under U.S. law, for United States agents to carry out kidnappings anywhere in the world. And a presidential executive order has specifically authorized U.S. agents to do this.

An extreme example was reported in *The New York Times Magazine* for Sunday, April 4, 1993. In this case U.S. agents not only kidnapped a woman from Venezuela, but arranged for

Venezuelan authorities to destroy all records of her Venezuelan citizenship and passport — on the assumption that they were illegally acquired. (Whether or not they were is unknown.) Incidentally, the woman was sentenced to 32 years in federal prison for money laundering, so she won't be challenging the Venezuelan authorities for some time.

Much more common than an actual kidnapping is to simply prevail upon the government concerned to deport the person as an undesirable alien. Unless the person is always in their country of second citizenship, almost any government will cooperate in such a request rather than get its court system involved in a long and expensive extradition case over a visiting alien. This can happen even in the country of the second citizenship in two ways. The first is that if the person enters his second country of citizenship on his first country passport, then for that visit he is usually treated solely as a citizen of the first country — after all, that was his claim at the time of entry. The second is that a powerful government, such as the U.S., may prevail on the second citizenship country to cancel the citizenship. This can be done particularly easily if it is a bought citizenship and a case can be made that it was bought with criminal proceeds.

Revoking a citizenship by marriage is harder, although theoretically it might be possible if the government that granted the citizenship were to claim that the marriage was a sham for the purpose of acquiring citizenship.

Least likely to be revoked is a citizenship acquired by inheritance, as in most countries this is a fundamental right that is irrevocable.

The one exception to the ease of extradition is that many countries prohibit the extradition of their own citizens, either by statute or by a clause in the constitution. Of course such a clause does nothing to protect one against kidnapping, as happened recently with a U.S. government kidnapping of a Honduran national. The Honduras constitution prohibits extradition of its citizens. Whether U.S. agents would be as likely to try a kidnapping in Copenhagen or Paris is — so far — an untested question.

The concept of extraditing a citizen is most common in the Anglo-American legal system. At one time a warrant issued in a Commonwealth country was valid anywhere in the Commonwealth, on the theory that it was all one legal system under Her Majesty The Queen. Although most Commonwealth countries today do have an extradition procedure, it is still often the same as the token extradition that exists between states of the U.S. So the concept of easy extradition of its own citizens eventually worked its way into the legal systems of most countries that inherited the British legal system — the U.S., Canada, Australia, etc.

Under Brazilian law, Ronald Biggs, one of the perpetrators of Britain's great train robbery, was able to escape extradition by the simple (and probably pleasant) tactic of fathering a baby born in Brazil. Publicity over the event has led to some misconceptions about the ease of acquiring Brazilian nationality. Brazilian citizenship is fairly difficult to obtain. Biggs was able to take advantage of a clause in the Brazilian constitution which prohibits the extradition or deportation of the father of a Brazilian-born child while he is supporting that child. But it does not grant citizenship under that clause, and the protection ends when the child turns 18 and is presumably no longer being supported by the father.

For those who remember various Wall Street scandals of the '50s ending in the crook fleeing to Brazil, bear in mind that Brazil now has an extradition treaty with the U.S.

Most of the civil law countries of Europe prohibit the extradition of their own citizens — France, Germany, the Netherlands, Switzerland, and Denmark are all examples. The Germans interpret this clause of their constitution so strictly that when a German criminal serving a prison sentence in Italy escaped and returned to Germany, Germany refused to extradite him.

In theory political offenses are not extraditable, but what is political can be hard to define. Tax offenses are also generally not extraditable, but fraud is, so a government wishing to pursue a tax case may convert it to a case of tax fraud.

Chapter 12
Of Passports And Nationality — Some Practical Reminders

A s a U.S. citizen with a second nationality, you must observe the U.S. law on passports. U.S. law DOES NOT PROHIBIT dual nationality. You are not allowed to use your foreign passport to enter or leave the United States. An American cannot have a U.S. visa in his foreign passport. Similarly, if you have a foreign passport, you usually must use it to enter or leave that foreign country, but laws on this vary widely from country to country.

Prudence dictates that you should never tell an official at the border of any country that you have more than one passport — particularly not a customs officer or border guard. Your position may be perfectly legal, but such complexities are generally beyond the understanding of the low level civil servants who man the border posts. Once your passport has been seized, even if the law is on your side, you will have to spend time, legal fees, and agony getting it back.

Complying with the rules of both countries whose passports you hold can get tricky. For instance, if you are a U.S.-Brazilian dual national flying from Rio de Janeiro to New York, show your U.S. passport when getting a boarding pass at the airline counter, because your Brazilian passport does not have a U.S. visa. (No airline will fly you to the United States if it is afraid you will be stopped at the border and the airline will have to fly you back at their expense.) Then show your Brazilian passport to Brazilian exit control as you leave Brazil, because your U.S. passport does not have a Brazilian visa. On your flight, put away the Brazilian passport and get ready to show the U.S. one.

Protecting Your Passport

You should never give a passport to a foreign official asking you for proof of identity in relationship to something other than admission to his country. For example, if you are asked to provide proof of your identity for a traffic or parking offense abroad, hold the passport firmly in your hand while the cop writes down the information on it. If you let him take the document, he may refuse to give it up unless you appear in court and plead — perhaps many days or weeks later. The Embassy of the United States (or any other country) will not be able to help you get it back; and for reasons of good relations with the host country, it may refuse to grant you a new passport right away. (Having a lot of traffic accidents may be a good reason to have a second passport.) To avoid ruining your holiday plans, you will have to post a bond, costing many times the likely fine for what you have allegedly done, to get your passport back.

An American "green card," or resident's alien registration card, is granted to an alien who has the right to live and work in the United States. It is normally issued to a resident alien who has entered the country with a visa granted by the United States in a passport issued by another jurisdiction. In cases where the alien returned to his own country and his passport was seized by the authorities, his "green card" was sufficient to get him back into the United States.

Chapter 13
Nationality For Sale

A number of countries are in the business of selling citizenship — or what amounts to it. Before you get into a situation such as this, remember that the terms are subject to change with the political situation, and, what is more worrying, the recognition of passports previously purchased is also an issue.

The Caribbean's offshore centers have been arguably the most accommodating of all jurisdictions to the widespread fears about Hong Kong's status after June 30, 1997.

Many Caribbean islands are now selling citizenships — often specifically targeting Hong Kong's wealthy who are understandably jittery over the coming amalgamation of Hong Kong capitalism with Chinese government jurisdiction.

Dominica, for instance, in the eastern Caribbean, has put its citizenship up for sale, offering passports to "new economic citizens" in exchange for investment.

The new Dominican citizen pays the government $25,000, which goes into a trust fund. They will also be required to make an initial business investment of not less than $35,000 in an export producing venture employing locals.

The twin islands of St. Kitts-Nevis are also hoping to inject a little more high net worth into their 50,000 population. They plan to allocate several hundred passports to Hong Kongers and 3000 "economic citizenships" to other potential applicants.

Nor is Jamaica averse to highly liquid applicants. It will give preference to people who can commit no less than $100,000 to ventures creating local jobs.

International Recognition of Acquired Nationalities

All nationalities are not created equal. Under international law, some nationalities are treated as frivolous. You should be aware that dual nationality may not be worth very much legally if it was acquired for cash. Before you go to all the trouble — and expense — of acquiring a second nationality, you should make sure it will do you some good once you've obtained it.

The key case on this issue was heard by the International Court of Justice in the Hague in 1955. The Nottebaum case involved a German-born claimant to Liechtenstein nationality, who sought damages for expropriation from Guatemala. Guatemala challenged Mr. Nottebaum on the grounds that he had been naturalized under provisions of Liechtenstein law on nationality that were not in conformity with international law. The naturalization did not require any previous residence in the country of Liechtenstein, for example.

Guatemala noted that Mr. Nottebaum, aged 58, had been given Liechtenstein nationality in absentia one month after the start of World War II, which had made it possible for him to avoid laws against Germans doing business in Guatemala.

Liechtenstein argued that international law does not require residency in the naturalizing state. The court, however, ruled for Guatemala, stating that Mr. Nottebaum's naturalization "lacked the genuineness required for establishing the link of nationality between a person and a state."

There was no residence requirement. Liechtenstein added one subsequently, and incidentally made it much more difficult to become a Liechtensteiner unless you are descended from one.

Nationalities granted without any residence requirement are therefore suspect under international law. That does not mean, however, that they are useless in other circumstances.

This is not the same as nationality without residence that might be acquired because you had a parent born in the country or you married a citizen of that country. Those family ties give you a link to the country that is not present in a purchased nationality. A nationality available by mere exercise of the checkbook is suspect under international law. Most countries selling citizenships now try to get around this precedent by creating a substantial tie with the country — a significant investment in the country, a waiver of residence requirements for making that investment, etc. No government simply sells citizenship outright. Since the U.S., Canada, and Australia have now created their own "investor-immigrant" categories, the principle of citizenship for investment is much less likely to be challenged in international law, even though some of the countries are accepting a token investment of $20,000 or so in a government bond, or a time-share in a citrus grove.

Information on countries "selling" citizenships is such a rapidly changing field that it is impossible for us to give you full details. Some examples of current possibilities follow. There is one publication that is revised frequently, and which covers the field of citizenships. *The Passport Report* is published by Scope International Ltd., Forestside House, Forestside, Rowlands Castle, Hants., PO9 6EE, Great Britain. They will send a free catalog on request.

The book you are reading now emphasizes the more permanent routes to citizenship — ancestry and marriage — areas in which the laws change slowly. Before purchasing any second citizenship, it is particularly useful to check your immediate family tree to see if you have any citizenship already that you are unaware of. It is not uncommon.

Having said that, there are still many times when purchase is the only method available. In many cases, the nationality is being sold to families (father, mother, and all children under 18) for the single fee.

Chapter 14
Practical Second Nationalities For Americans — And How To Acquire Them

Dual Nationality by Birth

One of the best ways for an American to get a second nationality is to discover that he already has one and didn't know it. Some of the more common countries are discussed here, which will also give you an idea of the vast differences in citizenship laws between countries. It is important to check the details with any country to which you might have a tie through descent or marriage.

There are several general categories of citizenship laws. Some countries grant automatic citizenship to the child of a citizen, regardless of where the child is born, and that citizenship is permanent. Germany, France, and Ireland are examples of this. Some do so only if the child is registered at a consulate of the country within a certain time after birth — two years for Venezuela, for example.

Some grant automatic citizenship at birth, but if the child is still living outside the country at age 21 he must register with the consulate his intention to retain citizenship — and for some countries, every ten years thereafter. Switzerland has this type of law.

A number of Latin American countries do not grant automatic citizenship at birth, but if a foreign-born child of a citizen takes up residence in the country he is automatically a citizen — Chile and Colombia are examples of this.

Nationality by Marriage

If you are able and willing to be married, you can get many nationalities instantly or more rapidly than otherwise (although despite U.N. rules, many of these laws are sex-biased). Some countries (notably Thailand) object to their women marrying foreigners and make it difficult to acquire nationality thereby, and many countries allow a woman to take up her husband's nationality immediately — but not the reverse. A woman can instantly acquire her husband's nationality if he is from: Andorra, Argentina, Israel, Lebanon, Liechtenstein, Malta, Monaco, New Zealand, Norway, Panama, Portugal, St. Kitts (formerly St. Christopher), Saint Lucia, Switzerland, Thailand, or Turkey. A man can acquire his wife's nationality in fewer cases, if she is from: Israel, Lebanon, Panama, Portugal, St. Kitts, Saint Lucia or Turkey.

Furthermore, many countries reduce residence requirements for the spouses of their nationals who want to acquire citizenship. These countries include, beginning with sex-neutral countries: Austria, Belgium, Bermuda, Bolivia, the Channel Islands, Denmark, Finland, France, Germany (in the case of a spouse who acquired nationality by birth only), Ireland, Italy,

Luxembourg, the Netherlands, New Zealand, Norway, Panama, Portugal, Spain, St. Kitts, Switzerland, Turkey, the United Kingdom (in the case of a spouse who acquired nationality by birth only), the United States, and Venezuela. Countries that reduce residence requirements for foreign wives when they do not grant these ladies instant citizenship include: Cyprus and the Dominican Republic.

Citizenship from Ancestry

You also can acquire citizenship by remote ancestry. Some countries, such as Turkey, do not recognize foreign naturalization of their citizens. So even many generations from one's Anatolian beginnings, it is very easy to be granted Turkish citizenship. Turkish consular officials are authorized to give it instantly to people who can prove that they are Turkish by ancestry. You should be able to speak Turkish, if only a few words. Turkey (according to Turkish consuls) can be taken to include lands Turkey lost at the end of World War I or even earlier, even though under international treaty, persons residing in the new countries carved out of Turkey in 1918 are deemed to have become nationals of the new countries.

Nationality by descent is available to those who can prove ancestry (normally back to their grandparents) in Belize, Italy and Ireland. It is also available in special cases to people of German descent. The child of one British-born parent usually can claim British citizenship. Only Ireland and Belize give nationality without any other requirements, such as residence, to anyone who has at least one native-born grandparent. Germany gives current refugees or those descended from refugees citizenship without a residence requirement.

Israeli nationality is transmitted *jus sanguinis* forever. A child who has only one Jewish parent is considered Jewish on condition that his mother is Jewish. This nationality law is based on Jewish religious law which defines a Jew in this way. Israel does not require that you renounce your previous nationality and grants its citizenship automatically to those deemed by the rabbis to be Jews, children or grandchildren of Jews, or spouses of Jews.

Of course, giving the rabbis so much power has resulted in injustice: banning a Catholic monk of pure Jewish extraction from Israeli citizenship (because the rabbis do not count converts to Christianity as Jews); making the Ethiopian Jews fight for automatic citizenship (which they eventually got); denying automatic citizenship to some Indian Jews, because they practice caste discrimination (the B'nei Israel of Cochin) while granting it to other Indian Jews from Bombay, who do not; rulings attempting (so far unsuccessfully) to deny Israeli nationality to the children of women converted to Judaism by reform and conservative rabbis (the rabbinical judges in Israel are all orthodox).

EU Rules Create a de facto Common Citizenship

The 12 nations of the European Union gave up part of their sovereignty. Under international law, sovereignty includes a country's right to make anyone it chooses a citizen; it also includes the right to refuse admission to anyone who is not a citizen. Individuals who are citizens of any of the EU countries are allowed to enter, to live, and to work in any of the others.

The 12 countries of the EU are: the United Kingdom, Ireland, France, Italy, Germany, Spain, Portugal, Greece,

Denmark, the Netherlands, Belgium, and Luxembourg. (Austria, Finland, and Norway are likely to be members by the time this book is published.) As a result, acquiring the citizenship of any one of these countries is almost the legal equivalent of acquiring citizenship to all of them. Already, no visa requirements are imposed within the EU. Countries that still require visas grant them automatically at the border to other EU citizens; and countries still requiring residence permits for foreigners do not charge for these permits when the applicant is from an EU country. In practice, anyone with a residence permit from an EU country can cross land frontiers with no passport at all. Identity cards or residence permits issued by one EU country are usually sufficient for entry to another EU country.

The first major effect of this has been to make it more difficult to acquire some EU nationalities, particularly through what may be called colonial preference. Britain has had to stop automatically admitting folks from the Commonwealth who are presumed white, such as Canadians, Australians, and New Zealanders. Spain and Portugal are under pressure to cease granting automatic residence and accelerated citizenship to Latin Americans. The argument, as usual, is that there are drug dealers among the Latin Americans who have settled in Spain and are now able to move freely within Europe north of the Pyrenees as a result. The effect may be to close a door that makes some acquired Latin American nationalities particularly advantageous. A bought Bolivian or Dominican passport (the process is described below) today can give you the right of domicile in EU Europe, because it gives you access to Spanish citizenship with a dramatically shortened residence requirement.

Spain has called on the EU to grant a common European citizenship and give people greater rights when they settle in member countries other than their own. The Spanish government has suggested to the EU that citizens of any member country should have the right to work in the public service of any other country, to vote in local elections, and to vote in elections for the European parliament in any country.

Great Britain

British nationality is obviously the second nationality most advantageous for Americans. Britain shares the same language. Americans often have British relatives. Britain is a member of the EU, so with a British passport, you in effect have a work permit for 12 European countries.

It is possible for an American to acquire British nationality. And the British do not require that you give up your previous nationality when you adopt theirs (unlike the United States). Furthermore, the British do not tell Washington what you have done.

The best way for an American to become British is to marry a British subject born in Britain. You then have the right to become British in three years instead of the usual five. And you can conveniently forget to tell the U.S. authorities what you have done. Your children, wherever they are born, can be dual nationals, too, simply by registering their birth (in theory within a year; in practice you have until they are at least 18) with the British Consulate.

Another useful way to acquire British nationality is to be born in Britain. Officially, being born in Britain does not make you British — but in practice it usually does. As an added incentive, Britain also offers cheap obstetrical care under the

National Health Service. But keep in mind that the people at customs are quite capable of turning away pregnant foreign women.

Take heart. The borders of Britain are extensive. A British-registered ship is part of Britain. (A U.S.-registered ship is part of the United States only if it is in U.S. territorial waters. A baby born on board a British ship in U.S. territorial waters is automatically a dual national — something to note during your next cruise.) The analogy appears to cover airplanes, but unfortunately, airlines will not let women on board after their seventh month of pregnancy. (You could try wearing a very large raincoat.) In general, it is helpful to establish British residence early in your pregnancy, or before you become pregnant.

If one of your children is born in Britain, he may also be granted British nationality retroactively. This is an example of *jus soli* in the case of a country where theoretically it is not practiced.

The offspring of recent British arrivals in the U.S. (notably war-brides) in many cases have successfully obtained British nationality, including the right to live and work in Britain or any other EU country.

On the other hand, people with British passports who are not of British parentage and were born outside Britain can be treated as something less than a full-fledged Briton. That is why you should become or marry or be descended from a Briton *born* in Britain.

Furthermore, expatriating acts for persons whose British nationality was acquired outside Britain, in cases where neither parent was British by birth or by naturalization, can be trivial or maddening.

It used to be one of the more popular citizenships, but British citizenship laws have become very restrictive, and the number of people eligible has shrunk. Some experts claim that good London lawyers can sometimes get you through the hurdles even if the British Embassy or Consulate in the U.S. says you are not eligible. Such is likely to be possible, but is beyond the scope of this book.

The British Embassy is reluctant to give out hard and fast rules, and prefers to discuss each case individually. In general British nationality will only apply if a parent was born in Britain, and until recently only the father counted. Like the Italians, it is critical that the parent not have given up their British nationality, before the birth. The answer varies considerably depending upon the year of your birth, and the dates and places of your parents' birth. If you are of direct British descent it is certainly worth exploring your situation with the nearest British consulate. It is certainly one of the most useful second citizenships to have.

Ireland

Taking a second nationality is not expatriating for Irish citizens. To decide who its people were after independence was won, the Republic of Ireland adopted a pure version of *jus sanguinis*. The Anglo-Irish or people from the Ulster counties could claim Irish citizenship if they wanted to, as could members of religious minorities. For years, the Chief Rabbi of Ireland marched in New York's St. Patrick's Day Parade. So you do not have to be Catholic.

Britain only recognized Irish nationality in 1948 and gave people born in Ireland one year to declare their loyalty to Britain either in the northern counties or on the mainland.

Many of them did but kept their Irish passports, too, as they were legally allowed to.

Irish passports are granted instantly on the basis of *jus sanguinis* to anyone with at least one Irish grandparent. You do not have to fulfill any residence requirements. And an Irish passport can be a useful document — in the case of U.S. journalists traveling to Cuba, for example, or White House officials (such as Robert McFarlane, a former National Security Advisor to Ronald Reagan involved in Irangate) traveling to Iran.

Many Americans can trace their ancestry to Ireland, and therefore can claim Irish citizenship. The Irish ancestor must be at least a parent or grandparent.

The language of Ireland is English, and there are a great many Americans with at least one Irish grandparent. Because Ireland is a member of the EU, obtaining an Irish passport is particularly valuable for those wishing to live or work anywhere in Europe.

The first point to bear in mind about Irish law is that the Irish constitution claims Northern Ireland to be part of the Republic of Ireland. Thus, although it is occupied by Britain, for most people born before 1922 in Northern Ireland they were Irish by birth. If this applies to your parent or grandparent you are in. (Certain persons born there after that date may also be able to qualify, but that is too complex for this book.) So if you always assumed your grandparents were English, you might check the birth records to find out if they really meant England — or if in fact they were born in Ulster.

If a parent was born in Ireland, you are deemed to be Irish by birth and need not register to acquire Irish citizenship. You simply take the documentation to the nearest Irish embassy or consulate and apply for an Irish passport. Generally you will be asked for your birth certificate, your parents' birth certificates and your parents' marriage certificate.

If you have an Irish grandparent, the procedure is a little different. You are not automatically a citizen, but must register your citizenship. This is done by producing all of the documentation (relevant birth and marriage certificates) to either an Irish embassy or consulate, or to the Ministry of Foreign Affairs in Dublin. Technically this is an application for registration in the foreign births record book. Once this has been done you are able to apply for a passport. So even if you don't want to apply for an Irish passport immediately, if you are entitled to this registration it is a good idea to do so immediately in case the law changes sometime in the future.

The other route to Irish citizenship is by marriage. A person married to an Irish citizen for three years or more is entitled to Irish citizenship simply by registering with the Irish embassy or consulate. Thus, if your spouse had an Irish parent and you have already been married for three years or more, all you have to do is register. But if your spouse had an Irish grandparent but has never registered as a citizen, then they must first get registered on the foreign births register and wait three years.

If you or your spouse have an Irish parent, you should register your children immediately. Should the law change, it may be very valuable to them sometime in the future.

France

In theory the French do not want dual nationals and expect you to renounce your other nationality upon becoming French. However, you do not have to take an oath, as when acquiring U.S. citizenship. And in practice, acquiring French citizenship does not jeopardize any other nationality you may have. In practice, anything goes. And almost nothing you do will remove unwanted French nationality once acquired — even if it was granted you through no action by you or your parents.

As a *jus sanguinis* country today, France does not grant its nationality automatically to those born in France. Automatic right to French nationality is given to anyone born of a French father after 1889; of a French father who resided in France after 1921; of a French father who served in the French army after 1959; of a French father no matter where he lived after 1945; of a French mother who lived in France after 1927; and of a French mother no matter where she lived after 1945.

In theory, only the offspring of a French mother or father, foundlings, or the offspring of foreign parents, at least one of whom had French nationality in the past, may become French under law by the mere fact of being born in the country. Otherwise, if you are born in France, you must reside there for at least 16 of your first 18 years to be able to declare yourself French and be granted citizenship. (If you are a boy, remember that becoming a French citizen makes you eligible for the draft; however, even refusing to serve in the military is not expatriating for someone who otherwise would be French.) In theory, citizenship is not granted to those born in France who move to another country. In theory, it is not granted to the children of those in France because of temporary assignment, because they are diplomats or foreign correspondents. But here, too, the practice is much sloppier than the law would lead you to believe.

The main reason is that French border controls, until the recent crackdown on terrorists tightened matters up, were extremely maladroit. No one necessarily had his passport stamped upon entering or leaving the country, particularly not if the destination was another EU country. So the French have

been unable to verify residence requirements for citizenship —
and simply have ceased trying to do so.

In fact, if you are born in France to parents who are not
French, and your birth is declared at a French *mairie* (as it must
be before the parents can then proceed to the U.S. embassy to
register the child's birth there), the French effectively consider
you a French citizen. You need do nothing else.

And it is very difficult to get rid of French nationality once
the French have decided you are entitled to it.

So if you want French nationality for your child, he need
never do more than be born in France. If you need further
incentive, consider that the rate of infant mortality is much
lower than in the U.S., and maternity care is cheaper. One of
only two hospitals outside the United States where you can use
Blue Cross or other U.S. health insurance is the American
Hospital in Neuilly near Paris. All this works best for girl
babies, who won't get drafted.

In general, you also can acquire French nationality — after
one year — by marrying a French *citoyen* or *citoyenne*. The
theory is that only those who lose their prior nationality by the
act of marriage to a French person can gain French citizenship
automatically after a mere year of wedded bliss. But in practice
the French do not check on this. No French official can
possibly be expected to learn about foreign laws and read in a
foreign language. Here, too, the French, by not requiring
expatriation when they grant nationality, are creating dual
nationals.

You can also become French with as little as three years'
residence (five years is more usual) in France on condition that
you support yourself; but it is difficult to get a job because
foreigners are not given *cartes de travail*. Of course, if you
have the right to work in France because you are an EU

national or resident, you can acquire French nationality in addition to your other EU nationality or right of residence. Furthermore, if the French think you are worthy for some reason (for example, if you are a Nigerian from the former Biafra territory who works for a French company in Zaire; or a Chinese executive of a French company in Hong Kong), nobody imposes the residence requirement. If you have a parent born in France, you are a French citizen. Citizenship derives from either the father or the mother. When a child is born abroad, the parents are supposed to register the birth with the French consulate. But if this was not done, you may still apply for a "Certificat de Nationalite Francaise" by applying in French, with all supporting documentation, on an official application form which you may obtain from the nearest French consulate. The form is then submitted by you directly to Paris, and the wait for processing is about a year.

A common route to French citizenship is through marriage to a French citizen, either in France or abroad. The citizenship law is now gender neutral, so this works for anyone. The application for citizenship can be filed immediately, and the French government has one year to object to the naturalization. A brief test of knowledge of the French language is also required. There is no residence requirement — all of this may be done at the nearest French consulate. The French government is becoming concerned at the number of marriages of convenience however, so the regulations may change, or the examination of the citizenship within the one year period may become more rigorous. Our underground sources inform us that Paris prostitutes currently charge $3500 for a marriage of convenience, including a pre-nuptial agreement and a divorce once the citizenship becomes effective. (Sex is not included in the price, but legal fees are.)

For those willing to take a few language lessons, a French marriage of convenience is one of the quickest ways to a European citizenship. There are reportedly cases of couples who have divorced, contracted French marriages of convenience, then after acquiring the French citizenship and divorces from the partners of convenience, remarried.

Canada

Being born in the Commonwealth (or Ireland) will serve as no advantage for you in getting Canadian nationality by descent; however, naturalization is easier if you are a Briton. The advantages for an American of becoming Canadian are minimal, unless he wants to live in Canada. (Although in earlier periods, some individuals managed to avoid the draft by heading north of the border.)

If you become Canadian, give up your U.S. citizenship, and live in a third country, Canada, unlike the United States, will not tax you on your worldwide income, which is an advantage. (However, if you are naturalized and spend 10 years outside Canada, you may be expatriated — stripped of your citizenship — at the discretion of the government.)

Another advantage is that Canadians are allowed to enter Britain as Commonwealth citizens without having to have a prior visa. Americans should not despair about the possibility of acquiring dual nationality by birth in Canada or the United States, however. A Canadian father or mother can transmit nationality to a child born in the United States; a U.S. mother or father can transmit nationality to a child born in Canada. Because both also practice *jus soli*, the single largest group of American dual nationals in fact are precisely these kiddies.

Canada has a three year residence requirement for citizenship, after admission as an immigrant. The difficulty is not obtaining the citizenship, but being admitted as an immigrant.

The most popular way at the moment is the investor visa category, which is being heavily used by Hong Kong Chinese moving to Vancouver. For as little as an investment of $250,000 and a three year wait, Canadian citizenship is possible.

The Canadian government is quite helpful in giving definite answers on whether you have Canadian citizenship through ancestry. Any Canadian consulate will give you a form, which you complete with personal history information, and submit with copies of relevant birth records to the Registrar of Canadian Citizenship in Ottawa. A "Certificate of Canadian Citizenship" will be issued if you are a citizen by descent, and this can be used to obtain a Canadian passport.

Canada is a rather special case. The law has been changed, first to make it more difficult for Canadians to become dual nationals (about the time of World War I), and then in 1977, to make it easier. What this means is that Canadians who became citizens of another country before 1977 may have lost their Canadian citizenship by so doing, but now have a chance to get it back again.

Complicating matters further was the change of law in 1947. Until that time, Canada did not recognize a woman's prior citizenship when she married a Canadian. Furthermore, it did not recognize her Canadian nationality when she married a foreigner. In the first case, involving a non-Canadian woman marrying a Canadian and thereby becoming Canadian, the woman's country of origin still might have considered her a national of that country. Furthermore, her country of origin also might consider any children she might have to be nationals as well.

Between 1947 and 1977, these women and their children were discouraged from becoming dual nationals by the severe Canadian laws against dual nationality. But under the Citizenship Act of Feb. 15, 1977, dual citizenship is allowed. If Canadians with the right to another nationality act now to assert their dual citizenship, they no longer risk losing their Canadian nationality for so doing.

Canadians who might have the right to another citizenship in the first instance should contact the embassy or consulate of that country in Canada. Because the law no longer prohibits Canadians from dual nationality, they have no reason to go to third countries or intermediaries.

Under the new law, those applying for Canadian citizenship often can retain their nationality of origin. They must decide on the basis of the possible advantages and disadvantages (considering such burdens as military service) if they want to retain the former nationality.

Similarly, a Canadian living outside Canada no longer automatically ceases being Canadian merely by gaining another citizenship. He must formally renounce Canadian citizenship by applying through a Canadian consular post. Of course, if he does so, the former Canadian may no longer use a Canadian passport; nor can he return as a permanent resident to Canada without going through immigration procedures.

Belize

Belize formerly had a program to grant citizenship in exchange for the purchase of a government bond. That program ended several years ago, and many believe that Belize citizenship is no longer easily acquired.

This is not the case, however. A new Belize government program began in February, 1992, again offering citizenships to people who invest in the country. (There had been some question as to whether the purchase of a government bond demonstrated a sufficient connection with the country under international law.)

The required investment and fees combined total $54,000 for a family and $44,000 for a single applicant.

There is no need for the applicant to leave the country where he is presently residing while the application is being processed. However, the government of Belize does specify that the applicant must visit Belize within five years of the citizenship being granted. Should the holder of the Belizean passport not visit Belize during this period the authorities will refuse to renew the passport after the original five year validity.

Belize is a full member of the British Commonwealth, and its official language is English. It is a rapidly developing country with a population of approximately 180,000.

Processing times are approximately eight weeks for the citizenship and another four weeks for the passport.

Bolivia

You can acquire Bolivian nationality at an accelerated rate by right of "meritorious service," according to the constitution and legislation. You need fulfill no residence requirement, and the entire family is covered. Meritorious service includes contributing funds to development projects and state-owned companies. If you contribute $20,000 to $25,000 you are considered a national benefactor and get citizenship and a passport.

An international attorney can help you deal with local lawyers, who will complete the paperwork for a fee. Bolivian passports are good for five years and must be revalidated every two years. They also can be renewed.

Ask around. There are many lawyers in this business, and the fees vary wildly. Twenty-thousand dollars is the figure heard most often.

The Dominican Republic

The Dominican Republic shares an island with Haiti. Its nationality law provides for instant naturalization for "immigrant settlers." Because no residence requirement is imposed on anyone applying for citizenship, you do not have to visit or live in the country, although you may want to. The island is very pleasant, and it is building up its tourism business. The naturalization process normally takes three months. Prices quoted were in the $20,000 range. As of early 1994 the Dominican Republic closed this door, and the citizenship cannot currently be acquired through purchase.

Ecuador

An Ecuadorian passport is available to an investor who deposits $1,000 and agrees to invest another $24,000 within 90 days of admission to the country as an immigrant. The investment can be in any industry. The theory is that meritorious service, such as investment, results in citizenship.

You have to reside in Ecuador while the processing takes place. It usually takes two to three months, after which you are free to leave with your new passport. You also have to provide a police certificate of good conduct. These are easily available from the authorities of almost any country you may have lived in, including the United States. However, the United States may take a very long time to provide this information, and you are billed for having the search accelerated and the results telexed instead of being sent by slow boat. For your information, Great Britain refuses to provide these forms (as a matter of principle).

Guatemala

The residency requirement (five years) in theory can be waived by the executive in cases of definitive ownership of some real property and possession of capital invested in real estate or an industrial enterprise (more than 20,000 quetzals, or about $5,000). These conditions may be waived in cases where "the alien has rendered the country important services or contributed to its development."

Mexico

Unlike many of its fellow Latin American countries, Mexico is serious about its nationality, and it is very difficult to obtain. Americans often think that Mexican citizenship can easily be bought, but in fact it is impossible to buy, and is listed in this section primarily as a warning not to be taken for a large fee by somebody claiming to be able to sell it to you. So there is no simple way to avoid the severe restrictions on acquisition of real estate in Mexico by foreigners. You cannot become Mexican easily. Mexican nationality law is strict. You can become Mexican if you are born in Mexico. Mexican ships and airplanes — even those traveling in international waters — are considered part of Mexico.

You lose Mexican nationality if you voluntarily take a foreign citizenship or a foreign title of nobility. The latter has been tested in the courts and has been refined to mean that you have agreed to submit to a foreign authority. Naturalized Mexican citizens can lose their nationality if they spend five years or longer continually in their countries of original nationality. You also can lose Mexican nationality if you obtain a passport that requires you to submit to a foreign government.

You cannot lose Mexican nationality by the mere fact of marrying a foreigner.

Throughout the 19th century, it was legal for Mexicans to enter the United States without having to meet the conditions imposed on other entrants, notably the need to prove literacy and pay $8. During both world wars, the United States, in need of cheap labor, encouraged Mexicans to enter the United States — by making the border easily penetrable and requiring no paperwork. It was only in the 1950s, under pressure from the unions, that the border began to be patrolled and *braceros* (contract laborers) and wetbacks turned back.

If you were born in the United States and your father or mother was born in Mexico and did not take up United States nationality because he or she entered the country illegally or at a time of free movement, it is possible for you to claim Mexican nationality. That is because you acquired U.S. nationality automatically and not voluntarily. You would not be subject to the residency test, because the government would not consider you a naturalized citizen.

Paraguay and Panama

Panama is for bird lovers. It has laws providing for instant naturalization of "immigrants who establish themselves in the country and devote themselves to work of agriculture, stock raising, the breeding of birds, and other similar industries." Paraguay provides for naturalization, after a shortened residence requirement, of those who "possess immovable or other property or who practice a science, art, or industry." The reality in both countries is that these laws are used as the legal basis for granting citizenship to those who buy it through agents and brokers with governmental connections.

Note that many Latin American countries also confer their nationality on foreign-born children of their nationals who come to live in the territory. This often applies both to those who have emigrated from the country in the past, and to the offspring (under age 18) of new citizens by naturalization.

Jamaica

Jamaica is offering passports to persons who have lived in a British Commonwealth country for five of the past seven years and who have money. The passport is available without residence requirements. The target is Hong Kong-Chinese, but an American who has lived in a Commonwealth country for the necessary period could qualify. You appear to need to purchase a zero-coupon 10-year bond for $30,000 cash (which turns into $100,000 at the end of that time, a return of 13%). You also need to make a $50,000 investment in a development project approved by the government. You may leave that money in escrow until the citizenship has been granted. Finally, you need to pay fees of $20,000, which is quite expensive.

St. Kitts and Nevis

The law here has gone through some recent changes. There are special provisions for investors, particularly those who buy real estate, but that route is extremely expensive — so outrageously so that it is not worth discussion. But leaving aside the citizenship for investors deal, one of the more intriguing clauses of the St. Kitts constitution gives an automatic and instant right to citizenship to the spouse of a citizen of St. Kitts. It is a small country, and finding a citizen to marry may not be easy, but it is one of the few countries that protects the citizenship rights of spouses in its constitution, instead of merely by statute, regulation, or custom.

Section 92 (1)(a) of the Constitution of St. Kitts and Nevis indicates that *any person* who is married to a citizen is entitled, upon application, to be registered as a citizen.

Mauritius

The Indian Ocean state announced citizenship with 12 months residence to those who come from the Commonwealth and speak English. Immediate citizenship is available in special cases. The usual residence requirement for non-Commonwealth folks is cut to two years for persons who "invested in Mauritius a sum of not less than 300,000 rupees." We have not had any additional information since this announcement was made a couple of years ago.

Turkey

Persons of Turkish origin can be declared Turkish by the Council of Ministers at the proposal of the Minister of the

Interior. In practice, Turkish consuls have the right to issue passports on the spot to those of Turkish descent. Also, those who "bring industrial establishments and who give extra-ordinary service in fields of social, cultural, economic, technical, scientific or artistic endeavor" may be granted citizenship. So, too, may those whom the Council of Ministers "judges it necessary to give Turkish nationality."

Turkish citizenship is also generally available instantly upon marriage, and is gender neutral, but the consulate will normally expect you to be able to speak Turkish.

Australia

Persons with money or skills are being encouraged to immigrate to Australia. The money part is considerable — A$500,000, or $350,000, which must be invested in Australia. The skills vary; among them is the ability to start a business that is considered desirable. Contact the Australian Consul in your home country for specific information.

You must by law reside in Australia for two years to be issued a passport; in practice it takes longer. However, if you have the specified A$500,000, you can get an instant residence permit but have up to four years, renewable to eight years, to fill the two-year requirement. You theoretically have to have spent the last year wholly in Australia, the reason being that Australia has a stiff tax on worldwide income of persons who are resident in the country for more than six months in a calendar year.

However, Australia has now got enough of an unemployment problem to have eliminated the program (dating from after WWII) whereby white Europeans were given free passage out if they looked like they were healthy and could work.

Those who merely have skills and not capital today must actually spend their time Down Under. Nor does Australia any longer subsidize immigrants, as it did until a decade ago. You also can no longer become Australian instantly by marrying one.

You are not required to give up your prior nationality upon becoming Australian, as its legal system is based on the British. Australian nationals have the right to enter Britain (no prior visa required); the reverse does not work. "Pommies" (the Australian slang for British) have to go through the two-year naturalization process just like anyone else. With the exception of New Zealanders, anyone wishing to enter Australia must have a visa.

Except for those making a large investment under the investor visa program, Australian residence is nearly impossible to obtain for those seeking employment in Australia. The domestic unemployment picture is so bad that Australia has no use for immigrants who just want to work there. There are still numerous pamphlets on the market discussing the ease of obtaining an Australian residency. They are about a decade out of date, and the Australian embassies are constantly issuing warnings not to be fooled by publications talking about getting jobs in Australia.

For entrepreneurs, however, Australia is so welcoming that they have recently run full page ads in American business publications seeking investor immigrants. They want only investors with a proven business track record.

New Zealand

New Zealand also offers a program for those with entrepreneurial ability, cash, or skills. Each case is treated on its merits. Investors with as little as $50,000 have a chance to qualify, but in reality a much more substantial investment is likely to be required.

You may also be able to become a New Zealander by marrying a Kiwi. As with Britain, you do not have to renounce prior nationality upon naturalization. And New Zealand requires visas for anyone coming into the country, with the exception of Australians. As is often the case, official information sources differ. The New Zealand embassy says becoming a New Zealander via the marriage route cannot be done, but contacts in New Zealand say it is done all the time.

New Zealand allows overlap with British citizenship to the greatest extent of all Commonwealth countries. A citizen of Britain (or the Republic of Ireland) by birth, naturalization, or registration can become a New Zealander after one-year's residence. A Briton marrying a New Zealander can adopt N.Z. (pronounced "enn zed") nationality with no loss of British nationality; a New Zealander marrying a Briton can do the reverse. An infant born in New Zealand with a British parent may be registered for British nationality with no effect on his New Zealand nationality; and an infant born in Britain with an N.Z. parent may be registered for N.Z. nationality with no effect on his British nationality. Not surprisingly, the largest block of dual nationals in New Zealand is also British. New Zealand, with the exception of Britain, is the only country that still practices Commonwealth preference.

For an American reader with an Irish grandparent, this becomes a quick backdoor to New Zealand. Or perhaps your spouse of three years or more has an Irish grandparent, in which case you can register as an Irish citizen and then use this method.

Italy

Another very popular second citizenship for Americans is Italian, because of the large number of Italian Americans and a relatively easy citizenship law.

If you were born in the United States you may also be considered an Italian citizen if any one of these situations pertains to you:

1) your father was an Italian citizen at the time of your birth and you never renounced your right to Italian citizenship;

2) your mother was an Italian citizen at the time of your birth, you were born after January 1, 1948, and you never renounced your Italian citizenship;

3) your father was born in the United States and your paternal grandfather was an Italian citizen at the time of his birth. Neither you nor your father ever renounced the right to Italian citizenship.

4) your mother was born in the United States, you were born after January 1, 1948 and your maternal grandfather was an Italian citizen at the time of her birth. Neither you nor your mother ever renounced the right to Italian citizenship.

If number one or number two applies to you, the following documentation must be obtained:

♦ your father's or your mother's birth certificate — write to the "comune" where your father or your mother was born and request his or her "Estratto dagli Atti di Nascita";

♦ your parents' marriage certificate — if the marriage took place in Italy follow the same procedure described above for the birth certificate, asking for the "Estratto dagliatti di matrimonio." If the marriage took place in the U.S. you must obtain a "long form" of their marriage certificate which is a certified copy of the license and the certificate of performing marriage;

♦ your birth certificate (in the long form showing your parents' places of birth);

♦ your parents' naturalization certificates or their valid Italian passports and U.S. "Alien Registration Cards." If these documents are not available, it is necessary that you submit a statement (Form G-639) issued by the U.S. Immigration and Naturalization Service, stating that according to their records your parents either were naturalized American citizens (date of naturalization and certificate number) or that they are still considered legal alien residents.

Proof of your parents' date of American citizenship is imperative. *If the naturalization occurred before your birth, you are not entitled to Italian citizenship.*

If number three applies to you, you should obtain your paternal grandfather's birth certificate from Italy, his marriage certificate, and all of the documents listed for number one... with the exception that instead of your father's naturalization certificate you will need your grandfather's naturalization papers, showing that he was naturalized after the birth of your father, whose "long form" birth certificate is also required. *If your grand-father was naturalized before your father's birth then neither your father nor you are eligible for Italian citizenship.*

If number four applies to you, you must obtain your maternal grandfather's birth certificate, his marriage certificate, and all the documents listed for number two, except for your mother's naturalization certificate, because in this case you will need your maternal grandfather's naturalization papers.

Your application for the verification of Italian citizenship will not be accepted if the documents listed above contain any errors in the spelling of names and/or dates recorded on them.

The application must be submitted to the Italian consulate having territorial jurisdiction for the state in which you were born — not the one where you now reside.

Italian Citizenship by Marriage

The Italian citizenship law No. 123/1983 states "The alien or stateless spouse of an Italian citizen acquires Italian citizenship when s/he has been residing within the territory of the Republic for at least six months or after three years from the date of the marriage if there has been no dissolution, annulment or cessation of civil effects and there is no legal separation." It further specifies: "Citizenship is acquired by Decree of the President of the Republic, upon the proposal of the Minister of the Interior, at the request of the person concerned submitted to the Mayor of the Municipality of residence or to the competent consular officer."

What all this means is a six months wait after marriage if you are living in Italy, or three years if you are living in the United States. In the latter case, as with an Irish marriage, you simply register at the consulate, and the Italian citizenship is yours. But the procedure is considerably more complex than the Irish registration three years after marriage.

Germany

Under the German Constitution a person who acquires German nationality may keep any other nationality he already had. Germany opened its citizenship to refugees from former German territories, such as Alsace, Lorraine, and the Balkan States after World War I. After World War II, Germans from territories incorporated into Poland were granted nationality automatically. Before the unification, West Germany also granted citizenship to refugees from East Germany and East Berlin.

A group of people born in Russia who never were given Russian nationality are the so-called Volga Germans, whom Stalin moved to Central Asia during World War II for fear of their disloyalty. These are political-religious refugees. Many descended from religious dissidents of the 18th and 19th centuries, who were invited to Russia by Catherine the Great. Many are cousins to American Mennonites and Amish. Having no nationality at all, they were able to avoid Russian military service, which many of them objected to on religious grounds. (In the 19th century, many of these Russian Mennonites were drafted all the same, which led to a second Mennonite wave of immigrants to the United States, Canada, and Latin American countries where they were safe from the draft). Because you needed a passport for internal travel in the Soviet Union, these people were kept from traveling within the Soviet Union as well as abroad. With the breakup of the Soviet Union, Germany has been concerned about the possibility of suddenly acquiring millions of these refugees who would be entitled to automatic German citizenship under the constitution. Since many of these people were deported from the Ukraine by Stalin, the newly independent Ukraine has offered to allow them to return and obtain instant citizenship. Germany is providing financial aid for those who do, in order to reduce the number who may move to Germany.

It is possible for people of German background who are not Volga Germans to benefit from special German procedures to give these stateless people accelerated rights to German citizenship. This is another variant of *jus sanguinis*. The system is being used by other ethnic Germans who do have a nationality — but one they don't like, such as Polish citizenship — to avoid the 10-year residence requirement for German citizenship. And the trick is also being used by Poles who do not speak German at all, but have a German name. There are lawyers in Germany who specialize in this racket; you can find their shingles in the area around the railroad station of any big city.

Under German constitutional law you can keep your prior nationality if you become German through these methods, as you are not applying for naturalization but merely claiming your existing German citizenship.

The German government will also give its nationality to people who, during the Hitler years, were stripped of their German citizenship for no reason other than being Jewish or of Jewish descent. At that time, anyone with at least one Jewish grandparent was stripped of German citizenship. The children of these people also may be able to claim German citizenship. The Germans are saying that *jus sanguinis* also applies to people who are wholly or partly German-Jewish by ancestry. Many Israelis who qualify prefer to travel with dark green passports with eagles on the cover rather than light blue passports decorated with Stars of David.

A German passport gives you the right to live and work anywhere in the EU. You do not have to renounce your prior nationality to qualify, and the German authorities do not tell the country of origin what you have done.

Apart from those who may have a historical claim to German citizenship, the simple answer for most people with a father who was a German citizen is that they first apply for a "German Certificate of Citizenship" by submitting an application form to the nearest German consulate. In addition to the form they will require the applicant's birth certificate, the father's birth certificate, and documents proving the German citizenship of the father.

The Netherlands

The Netherlands is an extremely liberal country, and since 1985 this liberality applies to its citizenship law as well. There are a great many ways in which Dutch nationality can be obtained.

Until January 1, 1985, Dutch nationality could only be obtained through the father. Since January 1, 1985, citizenship can be obtained from either the father or the mother. The place of birth is of no importance.

A foreign minor may obtain Dutch nationality if he is acknowledged by a Dutch national (or recognized without acknowledgment).

A foreign minor whose adoptive father or mother possesses Dutch nationality will obtain Dutch nationality on the day the adoption comes into force through Dutch law.

Foreigners born in the Netherlands and having resided there since, have the option to obtain Dutch nationality between the ages of 18 and 25. Foreigners, born in the Netherlands, stateless, and having resided in the Netherlands for a period of 3 years, may obtain Dutch nationality before they turn 25.

Naturalization in the Netherlands normally requires five years residence and knowledge of the Dutch language. However, the term of five years does not apply to:

a) former Dutch nationals
b) a foreigner who has been married for three years to a Dutch national (man or woman)
c) a foreigner over 18 who becomes the child of a Dutch national through acknowledgment, recognition or adoption.

The five-year term is reduced to three years for an unmarried foreigner in a lasting relationship of at least three years with an unmarried Dutch national. This clause was inserted specifically to cover gay or lesbian relationships, although it also can be applied to unmarried heterosexual couples.

The five year term is reduced to two years for a person who has previously lived in the Netherlands for a period of at least ten years.

Austria

Austria is another one of the countries that holds possibilities for a number of Americans. Austrian citizenship may be obtained generally by origin, naturalization, or acceptance of a position as ordinary or extraordinary professor at an Austrian university.

A legitimate child obtains citizenship if the father or the mother is an Austrian citizen at the time of the child's birth. A child born out of wedlock obtains citizenship if the mother is an Austrian citizen at the time of birth.

The alien husband or wife of an Austrian citizen may be granted citizenship if:

◆ they have been married for at least one year and the alien husband/wife has established permanent residence in Austria for at least four years, or

◆ they have been married for at least two years and the alien husband/wife has established permanent residence in Austria for at least three years, or

◆ they have been married for at least five years and the husband/wife has been an Austrian citizen for at least ten years. This last option can be interesting if one's spouse is Austrian because of an Austrian parent, since it grants citizenship without a residence requirement. However, in the case of Austrian citizenship by marriage, Austrian law requires that the former nationality must be renounced.

Otherwise Austrian naturalization requires ten years residence in Austria.

Hungary

A good example of shifting desirability of a citizenship is Hungary. During the Communist era Hungarians would have given anything to get another passport. Now Hungary is suffering a wave of people from countries with worse passports trying to become Hungarian. This has come about because Hungarian law allows instant naturalization upon marriage to a Hungarian citizen.

According to Law No. 5 of 1957, a person living in marriage with a Hungarian spouse may be naturalized. Preference is given to applicants who are stateless or whose foreign citizenship has ceased, who terminated their foreign citizenship, or who request to be relieved of their foreign citizenship upon naturalization.

Of course if one is a refugee fleeing Haiti or Cuba, none of that seems too onerous. Because the Hungarian law is gender neutral, a number of African men have been seeking Hungarian passports. Those with a great deal of patience feel that Hungary is likely to be one of the first Eastern European countries to become a full member of the European Union, thus giving Hungarian citizens rights to live and work in the rest of Europe. (A similar argument has been made for Polish citizenship, and many American-born children of Poles are dusting off their long forgotten citizenship claims.)

Israel

The number of U.S. citizens taking out Israeli citizenship is high. In fact in 1992 the number grew 35% over the year before, while the number of new Israeli citizens from the former Soviet Union declined.

Under Israeli law, the acquisition of nationality is one of the few areas in which the law differentiates between Jews and non-Jews. The Law of Return grants every Jew the right to go to Israel as an *oleh* (Jewish immigrant), and the Israel Nationality Law automatically confers Israeli nationality on every *oleh* upon entering the country unless the *oleh* specifies otherwise. The law even provides that a Jew who expresses his desire to settle in Israel may be granted nationality by virtue of the Law of Return even before he physically immigrates, a clause which allows the Israeli government to issue travel documents to refugees in emergencies.

Article 4A of the Law of Return extends the Jewish rights to family members: "(a) The rights of a Jew under this Law and the rights of an *oleh* under the Nationality Law, 5712-1952, as well as the rights of an *oleh* under any other enactment, are also vested in a child and a grandchild of a Jew, the spouse of a Jew, and the spouse of a grandchild of a Jew, except for a person who has been a Jew and has voluntarily changed his religion."

The next section makes it clear that the family member need not even be living: "(b) It shall be immaterial whether or not a Jew by whose right a right under subsection (a) is claimed is still alive and whether or not he has immigrated to Israel."

Article 4B provides the definition of a Jew: "For the purposes of this Law, 'Jew' means a person who was born of a Jewish mother or has become converted to Judaism and who is not a member of another religion."

Section 5 of the law allows the Minister of the Interior to grant visas and citizenship to minors without their parents' consent, a section that has recently been used for minors from the Ukraine, Moldova, and former Yugoslavia who decided to flee without their families.

By contrast, an Arab or any other person not qualifying as a Jew under the Law of Return may acquire Israeli nationality in one of five ways detailed in the Nationality Law and summarized below.

1. *Nationality by residence in Israel.*

Subject to certain qualifications, this section of the law grants Israeli citizenship to former Palestinian citizens who are currently residents of Israel and have lived in Israel since its creation on May 14, 1948, or have entered Israel legally between that time and July 14, 1952, the date the Nationality Law went into effect.

2. *Nationality by birth.*

Nationality by reason of birth is given to any person whose father or mother was an Israeli national at the time of his birth. This provision holds true regardless of where the person in question may happen to have been born.

3. *Naturalization by birth on Israeli territory in addition to 5 years immediate prior residence in Israel.*

This provision grants Israeli nationality to persons who are born on Israeli territory who meet these qualifications: apply for Israeli citizenship between their 18th and 21st birthdays, have 5 consecutive years of residence in Israel immediately prior to filing a request for citizenship, have no criminal convictions for violation of security regulations, and have not been sentenced to jail for five years or more for violation of any other type of law.

4. *Naturalization.*

A person 18 years of age or older may acquire Israeli nationality by naturalization if he meets these criteria: (1) is currently in Israel, (2) has been in Israel for 3 of the 5 preceding years, (3) intends to settle in the country (4) has some knowledge of Hebrew (former Palestinian citizens are exempt from this provision), (5) renounces any and all foreign nationalities, and (6) takes an oath of loyalty to the State of Israel. Completion of all of the above requirements is not essential in all instances, however, as the Minister of the Interior at his discretion has the power (for a special reason) to waive requirements (1), (2),(4), and (5) above.

5. *By grant from the Minister of the Interior to certain categories of minors.*

The law provides, in addition, for a discretionary grant of citizenship to minors who are not Israeli nationals but who are residents of Israel.

It is important to note that the law discriminates in favor of Jews against all others only as to the *method* of acquiring nationality. In theory at least, once nationality has been acquired all Israeli nationals are treated equally.

A more detailed presentation of the Israeli citizenship process is available in *How To Immigrate To Israel and Obtain*

Instant Citizenship, published by Eden Press, Box 8410, Fountain Valley CA 92728. They will send a free catalog on request.

Saint Lucia

Now an independent country, the West Indian island of Saint Lucia is a member of the Commonwealth. A person born outside of Saint Lucia who had one Saint Lucian parent is a citizen of Saint Lucia.

Marriage to a Saint Lucian prior to independence only gave citizenship to a female, who was not required to pay an application fee.

The post-independence citizenship law is an interesting example of the asymmetry we spoke of earlier. Applicants, whether male or female qualify under Section 6 of the Citizenship of Saint Lucia Act. The application fee is applicable to all applicants, whether male or female. However, if the applicant is male, he must be resident in Saint Lucia at the time of application.

Apart from this immediate citizenship by marriage, regular naturalization requires seven years residence in Saint Lucia.

Uruguay — A Government Sponsored Second Passport Program

International Security Services, consultants in security matters and advisor to many governments worldwide, is screening investors for foreign investment in Uruguay. In appropriate cases the government would be prepared to grant passports, residency, and eventually citizenship, if the applicant purchases a ten-year interest-bearing government bond.

Uruguay has a population of about 3 million and the size is approximately 69,000 square miles, about the size of England and Wales, or Greece. It is one of the most stable countries in South America, and is a democracy with a liberal political regime.

It has a good climate, very beautiful scenery, and is the playground of wealthy Argentineans and Brazilians.

There is no personal income tax or capital gains tax. It has always been a good country for setting up tax haven corporations and bank accounts, as it has complete secrecy, like Switzerland. There are no currency restrictions.

The government would welcome foreign investors in banking and financial services, and there are many other business opportunities. Property is currently inexpensive.

The government of Uruguay is looking for bona-fide applications from the worldwide business community. In order to qualify for residency, a passport, and citizenship if desired, the applicant would have to buy a Uruguay government bond for $70,000 (U.S. dollars). Additional family members require a $10,000 Uruguayan government bond. The bonds pay 6.5% per annum, payable each year. The bonds are guaranteed by the Central Bank of Uruguay. At the end of ten years the bond is redeemable for the original capital, plus ten-year growth. The passport is permanent.

Applicants (and family members if appropriate) require the following documentation:
+ Certified copy of birth certificate;
+ Marriage certificate;
+ Health certificate for all family members showing that they are in good health and do not suffer from any communicable diseases;

- Professional reference from lawyer, minister of religion, or doctor, showing that they are respected members of the community;
- Bank reference;
- Police reference stating that they are respected members of the community, have no police record, and are not on any wanted list;
- Six passport photos, with negatives.

The whole transaction is handled through International Security Services, with the co-operation of the local Uruguayan consulate and their appointed legal representative. Currently most applications are being processed through London.

The total fees for disbursements, lawyers, preparation of government documentation, security and background checks, etc. are approximately $55,000 to $60,000, in addition to the $70,000 cost of the bond. The yield and growth from the bond will in fact repay all fees.

Therefore, the applicant acquires a passport that is universally recognized and which over the ten year period will have cost nothing. In addition, as the passport is universally recognized, visas will not be needed for most countries, with the major exceptions being France and the U.S.A., who require visas from nearly everyone.

Money is placed in escrow while the application is pending. Once all references have been cleared by International Security Services the applicant will be contacted and arrangements for purchase of the bond will be made at the Uruguayan Consulate. On the day the government bond is purchased the applicant/investor immediately gets a permanent residency certificate giving him the right to maintain a residence and business in Uruguay. Approximately 15 days after all the documents are lodged the applicant will get a passport and identity card. The residency and passport are permanent. If citizenship is desired, it can be had in approximately five to six months. Dual nationality is acceptable.

If, when International Security Services checks the documentation, it determines that the applicant would not qualify, then all money held by the escrow agent will be returned to the client except for a $1,000 handling fee.

To get information on this program, you should get in touch directly with International Security Services, Attn: Uruguayan Investor Program, 27 Old Gloucester Street, London WC1N 3XX, Great Britain. They can also be reached by fax at (44) 71 831 9489; Attn: Uruguayan Investor Program. It is best to give them some general information about yourself in your initial inquiry.

As we go to press, it appears very likely that the Uruguay government is going to enact an additional investor passport program, which will allow a person investing $100,000 into real estate in Uruguay to obtain instant citizenship. Information will be available from the same source cited above for the residence passort.

Opportunities in Eastern Europe and Former Soviet Republics

The most complicated laws on nationality are those of Russia, the Baltic Republics, other newly independent countries of the former Soviet Union, and Eastern Europe. And these laws are changing rapidly, as many of the countries are seeking ways to restore citizenship to those who lost it under the Communists and their descendants. So if your ethnic heritage includes ancestors from one of these countries, some first-hand research is in order. The situation is changing too fast for any book to be meaningful for long. You won't be alone in your inquiry — the embassies of these countries are being flooded with inquiries from former citizens and their children.

The new laws in these countries range from restrictive to extremely liberal. Estonia has excluded over half of its existing population from citizenship. Lithuania granted automatic citizenship to anyone who lived in the country during 1989 and 1990. Ukraine gave citizenship to everybody who lived in the country on the date of independence.

About the Author

Adam Starchild can occasionally be persuaded to take time off from his private entrepreneurial activities to write. During these interludes he has written over a dozen published books and hundreds of magazine articles, primarily on international business and legal strategies. His articles have a appeared in wide range of publications around the world, including *Business Opportunities Journal, Euromoney, International Living, The Futurist, Tax Planning International, Trusts & Estates,* and many more.

YOU WILL ALSO WANT TO READ:

☐ **61129 UNDERSTANDING U.S. IDENTITY DOCUMENTS,** *by John Q. Newman*. The most detailed examination of identity documents ever published. Covers birth certificates, Social Security cards, drivers licenses and passports. It shows how each document is generated and used, and explains the strengths and weaknesses of the agencies issuing them. An essential reference for anyone concerned with their official identity and how it is maintained and manipulated. *1991, 8½ x 11, 207 pp, Illustrated, soft cover.* $25.00.

☐ **10059 PERSONAL PRIVACY THROUGH FOREIGN INVESTING,** *by Trent Sands*. If you're frustrated with all the paperwork and taxes that burden the American investors, let Trent Sands show you how to safely and secretly move your dollars overseas. This book shows how to research foreign investment markets and set up an overseas back account. Covers: Switzerland, The Bahamas, The Cayman Islands, Bermuda, Great Britain, Australia, New Zealand, Luxembourg, Canada, And more. A world of opportunities for the privacy-conscious investor. *1993, 5½ x 8½, 72 pp, soft cover.* $10.00.

☐ **61127 REBORN OVERSEAS, Identity Building in Europe, Australia, and New Zealand,** *by Trent Sands*. The formation of the European Common Market has created a paper-tripping paradise. With an identity in any one nation, you can live, work and travel in all 12. This book shows how to get all the documents necessary to build a complete paper identity without leaving the United States and much more. *Sold for informational purposes only. 1991, 5½ x 8½, 110 pp, Illustrated, soft cover.* $14.95.

☐ **61114 REBORN IN CANADA, Personal Privacy Through a New Identity, Second Edition,** *by Trent Sands*. A complete guide to building a new identity in Canada from the ground up. covers birth certificates, drivers license, social insurance card, passport, credit cards, and much more. Learn how to thoroughly document your new identity without revealing any information about your former life. *1991, 5½ x 8½, 83 pp, Illustrated, soft cover.* $12.00.

Please check out our catalog ad on the next page for the very best in unusual and controversial books you will find anywhere. The catalog sells for $5. However, if you order any or all of the above titles you will receive it free.

··LOP95

Loompanics Unlimited
PO Box 1197
Port Townsend, WA 98368

Please send me the books I have checked above. I have enclosed $_____ which includes $4.00 for shipping and handling of 1 to 3 books, $6.00 for 4 or more. Washington residents include 7.9% sales tax.

Name_____

Address _____

City/State/Zip _____

Now accepting VISA and MasterCard.
1-800-380-2230 for credit card orders *only*.
Order Department hours 8 am to 4 pm Pacific time.